What people are saying about ...

GOD'S CRIME SCENE
FOR KIDS

"Detective Wallace has done it again! With wonderful stories and illustrations, he makes difficult concepts both interesting and understandable to kids. Hands down, it is one of the best apologetics resources for kids. We will definitely be using this book with our own children."

Sean and Stephanie McDowell, teachers,
author (Sean) of *Apologetics for a New
Generation*, and parents of three kids

"Christianity claims to be true. And we can believe this bold claim because a wealth of evidence backs it up. J. Warner and Susie Wallace do an excellent job of articulating the evidence in a way that kids (and grown-ups) can understand. This book will help the children in your life begin to see just how rational Christianity is as well as prepare them to withstand the inevitable attacks they will face."

Dr. Jeff Zweerink, astrophysicist,
scholar at Reasons to Believe, and
author of *Is There Life Out There?*

"The most important skill any investigator can possess, whether studying a crime scene or the natural world, is the ability to ask really great questions. In *God's Crime Scene for Kids*, J. Warner and

Susie Wallace provide not only an impressive collection of scientific facts but also a first-rate course in critical thinking for young people that is relatable, straightforward, and easy to understand without being oversimplified."

Sarah Salviander, astrophysicist, research fellow in astronomy at the University of Texas at Austin, and author of the *Astronomy and Astrophysics* homeschool curriculum

"God's Crime Scene is my go-to recommendation for anyone who wants to learn about the evidence for God's existence. I was thrilled to hear that a kids' version was coming out but honestly wondered how Detective Wallace was going to translate some of the more challenging scientific and philosophical concepts into material for eight- to twelve-year-olds. Now that I've read it, I'm blown away. This is brilliant! There's nothing else like it, and I'll be recommending it for years to come."

Natasha Crain, blogger, speaker, and author of *Keeping Your Kids on God's Side* and *Talking with Your Kids about God*

GOD'S
CRIME SCENE
FOR KIDS

GOD'S
CRIME SCENE

FOR KIDS

INVESTIGATE CREATION WITH A REAL DETECTIVE

J. WARNER WALLACE AND SUSIE WALLACE
WITH ROB SUGGS

David C Cook

transforming lives together

GOD'S CRIME SCENE FOR KIDS
Published by David C Cook
4050 Lee Vance Drive
Colorado Springs, CO 80918 U.S.A.

Integrity Music Limited, a Division of David C Cook
Eastbourne, East Sussex BN23 6NT, England

The graphic circle C logo is a registered trademark of David C Cook.

The website addresses recommended throughout this book are offered as a
resource to you. These websites are not intended in any way to be or imply an
endorsement on the part of David C Cook, nor do we vouch for their content.

LCCN 2017934395
ISBN 978-1-4347-1032-1
eISBN 978-0-8307-7202-5

© 2017 James Warner Wallace
Published in association with the literary agency of Mark
Sweeney & Associates, Bonita Springs, FL 34135.

Illustrations by J. Warner Wallace
The Team: Catherine DeVries, Rob Suggs,
Amy Konyndyk, Jack Campbell, Susan Murdock
Cover Design: Nick Lee
Cover Photo: ESO

Printed in the United States of America
First Edition 2017

3 4 5 6 7 8 9 10 11 12

083018

CONTENTS

WELCOME, CADETS

If you joined us for our prior investigation, *Cold-Case Christianity for Kids*, I'm excited that you're back again to help solve a new mystery. If this is your first time learning how to solve cases, don't worry. You're about to learn all you'll need to know to be a good investigator.

My name is J. Warner Wallace, and I'm a detective who investigates "cold cases"—crimes that remained unsolved for many years. Some of my cases have been on television and in the news. When I was a kid, I entered a cadet academy for young people who were interested in law enforcement. I learned a lot and eventually earned a graduation certificate. Years later, when I became a detective as an adult, I learned even *more* from my senior partner, Alan Jeffries. He taught me how to *think* like a detective. I owe him a lot.

I was intimidated by Detective Jeffries at first, because he was a very serious man who seemed a bit grumpy at times. But the more I got to know him, the more I realized he was a good man and a great detective. He's the perfect person to train *you* to solve a mystery with the other cadets in this book. The skills you'll learn from Detective Jeffries will help you solve cases and make other important decisions as well.

In fact, I used the skills I learned from Detective Jeffries to investigate the *Bible*. Although I am a Christian today, I wasn't always. I applied my detective skills to test what the Bible told me about Jesus. After I completed my investigation, I knew Jesus really was the Son of God.

I also used my detective skills to investigate the entire *universe*! I looked for clues the same way I do at a crime scene, and I tried to figure out what caused the universe and everything in it. I used every skill that Detective Jeffries taught me, and now you can do the very same thing. Alan Jeffries is about to teach *you*, along with the other cadets, how to investigate the universe as you solve a mystery involving a shoebox. In the end, you'll also be able to earn a graduation certificate of your own.

Your family can join the investigation. Just tell them to read the adult version of this book, *God's Crime Scene* (where they'll find *a lot* more detailed evidence), and go online to www.GodsCrimeSceneforKids.com to look at the leader's guide for each chapter. While you are there, be sure to check out the videos and activities my wife, Susie, and I created for you. Now, let's join the other cadets and solve a mystery!

J. Warner Wallace

The Mystery

"Did I just dream that?" Jason bolts upright in bed and looks at the ceiling. Did he imagine that loud crashing noise he heard overhead, or was it part of a dream? Could a noise in a dream actually wake someone from their sleep?

Jason rubs his eyes and looks at the clock on his nightstand: 2:30 a.m. What could cause such a noise at this time of night? The attic above Jason's head is hardly ever used, and he hasn't been up there in years. He grabs his flashlight from the nightstand drawer and slowly walks to the hallway. He flashes the light down the long, dark hall toward a partially open attic door.

He pushes past the half-open door and walks up the steps to the attic. Although he's scared at first, he reminds himself that he's a graduated cadet. What would the other cadets back at the Police

Department Junior Academy think if he was too afraid to explore his own house?

Jason gathers himself and tries to be calm as he enters the dark attic. He flips the light switch at the top of the stairs. The single lightbulb hanging in the middle of the attic blinks on, then makes a popping sound, and turns off once again. Jason toggles the switch off and on with no success. "Great," he whispers under his breath.

"Is anyone up here?" he asks, trying to sound confident and courageous. No response. He scans the attic with his flashlight. Dust particles swirl in the cramped space. There are lots of boxes, a mousetrap or two, a few dead bugs, and piles of old newspapers. Then Jason sees what might have been the source of the noise. On one side of the attic he observes a fallen stack of books. Thinking like a detective, he notices the dust around the books appears to be recently disturbed.

Jason moves in closer and peers at a slightly tattered shoebox lying among the books. Worn around the edges, it must have been stacked on top when the books fell. He uses the flashlight to examine the contents of the box. Minutes pass. Jason is so intrigued by what he discovers that he loses track of time ...

CSI Assignment:

Jason is trying not to be afraid as he explores the attic. Read Psalm 56:3, written by King David. When David was afraid, he put his trust in _____.

The next day, Jason enters the police briefing room and looks like he hasn't slept much. He squints under the bright lights and searches for his seat among the long rows of tables facing the front of the room. There's a small podium and a whiteboard in front of the tables, and the side walls contain information on local crime trends and wanted suspects. On the whiteboard, someone has written: "Special Investigation Junior Academy."

You're there along with other junior cadets, including your friends, Hannah and Daniel. Students from the local schools heard about this opportunity to train again at the Police Junior Cadet Academy. This time, the department is offering a Special Investigations course. You walk over to Jason to say hello, but before you can say anything, Detective Alan Jeffries enters the room.

"Take your seats, cadets!" Jeffries booms in his typical serious voice. If you didn't know better, you'd be a bit intimidated by his bear-like figure and the look on his face, but this is your *second* Junior Academy course with Detective Jeffries. He seems tough and businesslike, but you know he's as glad to see you as you are to see him.

Before Jeffries can say anything else, Jason's hand shoots up. "Sir," he says. "I've got a case!"

"A case of what? Measles?" asks Hannah.

Everyone laughs, but Jason says, "A case for us to solve."

"Let's hear it," says Jeffries.

"Well," Jason says, "I live with my grandma Miri. I was sleeping in my room last night and a loud noise woke me up. It came from above—in the attic. Hardly anyone ever goes up there, but I got my flashlight and went to see what made the noise."

"Yeah? Yeah?" says Daniel.

Jason describes the scene in the attic and the fallen stack of books.

"Okay, so what's the mystery? You already figured out what caused the noise," says Hannah.

"I found something mysterious under the fallen books."

"I found something mysterious under the fallen books." Jason describes the shoebox for the cadets. "At first I didn't think anything of it, but then I took a close look at what was inside." The cadets lean in as Jason recalls his findings. "I found a small hand shovel; a magnifying glass; an unmarked, graduation-type class ring; and a drawing of a boy standing next to a tall, unusual tree."

"That's weird," you say. "Those things don't seem to have much in common."

"It gets weirder," responds Jason as he removes an old piece of lined paper from his pocket. "This was also in the box." Jason reads the note:

Dear Jason,

If you're reading these words, good! The note got to you. Life is full of difficult situations and unanswered questions. No one knows that better than you. But I know where to find the answers. Follow these clues to find a gift just for you. It's the answer to all your questions. But you'll have to think carefully about the clues, dig around, look carefully, and change your mind.

"Now *that's* a mystery," says Hannah. "Is the note signed?"

"No," replies Jason.

"All right then," says Jeffries, "this is an excellent place to start our next Academy Course. I'll teach you a number of new investigative skills so you can solve this mystery. If you can apply these skills and figure out who wrote this note, you'll be eligible to graduate and earn your Special Investigations Certificate."

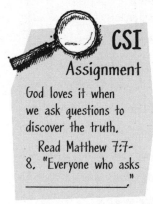

CSI Assignment

God loves it when we ask questions to discover the truth. Read Matthew 7:7-8, "Everyone who asks _____."

Everyone appears to be excited about the new "case." Jeffries walks to the whiteboard and gets everyone's attention. "Any initial observations about the note?" he asks.

Daniel, always thinking, says, "It said nobody knows about tough luck more than Jason. What does that mean?" Everyone pauses to think about this, then looks in Jason's direction.

Jason hesitates, then shares something he's never mentioned before. "I guess that's true," he says. He looks at the floor and adds quietly, "I lost my mom and dad when I was a baby. They died in a car accident. I don't remember them at all. Most people think my grandma Miri is my mom because she looks so young, I guess."

"So your grandmother raised you?" asks Hannah, placing a caring hand on his shoulder.

"Yes, it's just the two of us now. My grandpa, Ren, also died when I was about two years old. I've never understood why I had to lose my parents and grandfather before I even got to know them."

Listening to Jason, you think back to the other experiences you've had with him. When you first met him, he was one of the most skeptical people you'd ever encountered. He especially doubted the existence of God and the truth of Christianity. You wonder if his doubts were caused by his experience as a child. Did he question the existence of a "good" God because of what happened to his family members?

Dig Deep
Visit the Online Academy

Be sure to complete the Training Activities and Note Sheets.

Start assembling your Academy Notebook!

"So where's the box now?" asks Detective Jeffries.

"At home. I live just around the corner from the police department." Jason looks at Detective Jeffries. "I knew from my experience as a cadet that I should probably leave the box the way I found it and tell you about it today. I did tell Grandma about it, though. She thinks maybe Simba knocked the books and box over."

"Simba?" asks Hannah.

"Our cat. Also, Grandma recognizes the handwriting on the note. It's Grandpa Ren's writing."

"But what's that weird message about?" Daniel asks. "What are the clues your grandpa wrote about?"

Detective Jeffries says, "That's the mystery we're going to solve together, cadets." He focuses on Jason. "As we solve the mystery of the shoebox, I bet we can use our detective skills to find the other answers your grandpa was describing in that note too." Turning to the cadets, Jeffries instructs them, "Let's meet at Jason's house for our next session together."

Detective Jeffries walks up from around the corner and joins them.

Chapter One

How Did It Get Here?

Was the Universe an Inside Job?

The cadets are all present on the front porch of Jason's house, and it's time to start the next session. Detective Jeffries walks up from around the corner and joins them. He's carrying a professional-looking black workbag.

"So, where's the box?" Daniel asks Jason.

"Impatience is not a good detective skill," says Jeffries.

Daniel blushes. Hannah grins and adds, "We haven't even entered Jason's house yet!"

Jason opens the front door and is greeted immediately by Grandma Miri. She is a tiny woman with gray shoulder-length hair. She has a contagious smile.

"Welcome, everyone!" she booms. She's surprisingly loud for someone her size. "Jason told me all about your investigation. I'm excited to hear about what you may discover. Let me show you to the 'crime scene.'" She giggles a bit and escorts them to the attic stairwell.

"You must be Detective Jeffries," says Grandma Miri.

Jeffries politely extends his hand. "Thanks so much for allowing us to come here today."

Before Grandma Miri can respond, Simba appears and makes himself known with a loud *meeeow*. He's a sleek-looking orange tabby.

Detective Jeffries bends down and picks up the tabby.

Detective Jeffries bends down and picks up the tabby. "Nice kitty," he says as he rubs behind the cat's ears. Simba immediately snuggles in under Jeffries's neck and starts to purr. Jeffries cradles Simba gently for a moment. You smile as you recognize the often hidden, gentler side of the burly detective. Jeffries catches your smile from the corner of his eye and realizes all the cadets are staring at him as he's cuddling the cat. He quickly puts the cat down, regains his composure, and says sternly, "None of you saw that." Everyone laughs.

Light is now streaming through a small dormer window on one side of the attic. The space is rustic. Cobwebs can be seen in the open rafters. Not everyone can fit, so some of the cadets watch from the top of the stairs. The cadets take out their notepads to jot down their observations.

Detective Jeffries puts on a pair of evidence gloves and pulls out a digital camera from his black detective bag. "Let's start by photographing the attic the way you found it. Jason, is the attic about the same as it was when you came up last night?"

"I think so," says Jason, "but it was dark, and I hardly ever come up here."

Detective Definitions

Causation:

The act of causing something to happen or exist.

Detectives investigate evidence to figure out who or what caused the evidence to appear in the crime scene. If we don't know what caused the evidence to appear in the scene, it's much harder to solve mysteries.

Jeffries starts taking photographs of the fallen books and the shoebox. He also photographs the dusty area around the box, the cobwebs, and even the mousetraps lying on the floor of the attic. After several minutes, he turns to the cadets.

"This box," says Jeffries as he crouches down in the tight space, "is a good example of something I want to teach you today. One of the first questions an investigator asks, once he or she discovers what might be evidence, is: How did it get here? And Jason's mysterious shoebox is a great example."

He examines the box closely. "All right, cadets, what are we trying to solve in this investigation?"

The cadets look at one another for a minute, then you break the silence. "We're trying to solve a mystery about who put these items in the box, how they're supposed to be used, and what the note for Jason means, right?"

"Exactly," says Jeffries. "In order to answer those questions, we have to ask an important *first* question about *causation*."

"What's that?" asks one of the cadets.

"Well," responds Jeffries, "We need to figure out what caused the shoebox to be in the attic in the first place, and then what caused the items to be in the box."

Jeffries explains. "Imagine we're investigating a burglary at a local business and we find a glove at the scene of the crime. How do I know if it is an important piece of evidence? Maybe the thief dropped it. But if it just belongs to someone who works there (if it was there before the burglar even entered the scene), it's not actually evidence of the crime at all, right?"

"That makes sense," you say.

"Now let's turn our attention to the shoebox," says Jeffries, as he carefully lifts it from the floor. "Where did the box come from? There are really only two choices: the box came from somewhere *outside* the attic, or it was always *in* the attic."

"Always in the attic?" asks Jason. "That's crazy. I mean, it couldn't have *always* been here. Shoeboxes come from *somewhere*."

"But what if it sort of *grew* in here?" says Jeffries, with a little smile. You recognize that expression on Jeffries's face. You've seen it before when he's trying to get a response from the cadets.

Jeffries continues, "After all, mold grows in cellars, right? It just kind of happens *naturally*. Maybe *boxes* can grow in *attics*."

"Uh, I don't think so," says Hannah, with a bit of humor in her voice. "Shoeboxes don't grow in attics *naturally* … If they did, this attic would be filled with them, but this is the only one."

Detective Definitions

Explaining Evidence:

Giving a reason for a piece of evidence that exists in the scene.

When detectives investigate evidence, they ask, "Why did the evidence appear at the scene, and what does this tell us about the suspect (or whatever caused the evidence)?"

"Agreed," says Jeffries. "The box hasn't been in here forever, and it didn't appear here on its own. The same is true for everything *in the box*. Someone outside the attic put the shoebox in the room, and someone outside the box put these items inside."

Several of the cadets nod their heads in agreement.

Jeffries continues, "Now that we've answered that question, let's focus on what's inside the shoebox. Are there any clues *inside* the box that might tell us *what* or *who* the outside cause might be?"

"I think it is a *who*," says Hannah, "because there's a letter, and the letter *mentions* the things in the box. At least I think so. It reads, 'look carefully,' which could refer to the magnifying glass, and also, 'dig around,' which may be describing the shovel."

"Very good!" exclaims Jeffries. "Not only that, but Jason's grandmother says the note looks like it was written by Grandpa Ren."

"So we have good reasons to believe Grandpa Ren put those items in the box," says Daniel.

"Exactly," says Detective Jeffries. "We can't explain the things inside the shoebox with a cause that's *also* inside the shoebox. An *outside cause* is the best explanation, and so far, Grandpa Ren seems to be the most reasonable *outside cause*."

"Let's head back to the briefing room," says Jeffries, as he gently collects the box and places it in a paper evidence bag. "I bet we can apply this same approach to an important question about the universe."

 The *universe*? What did Detective Jeffries mean? You find yourself thinking about this as everyone returns to the police department and the cadets file back into the briefing room.

Once everyone is seated, Jeffries walks up to the whiteboard and draws a box.

"We live in a vast universe, filled with planets, stars, and galaxies. Everything in our universe is made up of space, time, and matter."

The cadets look a bit puzzled. What does this have to do with Jason's shoebox? Detective Jeffries sees the quizzical look on your faces and points to the box he drew on the whiteboard.

"We found some things in the shoebox and then tried to figure out if a cause *inside* or *outside* the box was the best explanation," explains Jeffries as he starts to draw the items from the shoebox. "What if we investigated the universe in a similar way?" Jeffries now draws a large diagram of the universe.

"Could the evidence we find in the cosmos have been caused by something *inside* the universe, involving nothing more than space, time, and matter? Or is the best explanation for this evidence something *other* than space, time, or matter; in other words, something *outside* the universe?

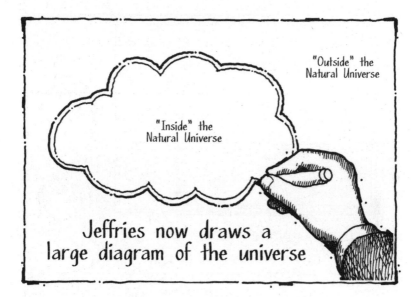

"Outside" the Natural Universe

"Inside" the Natural Universe

Jeffries now draws a large diagram of the universe

"The items in the box were either there forever, appeared there all by themselves, or were placed there by someone outside the box. In a similar way, everything we find in the universe has either been here forever, appeared here all by itself, or was placed here by something outside the universe."

Hannah gets an expression on her face like an idea just came to mind. "Something *outside* the universe that isn't made of space, time, or matter? Are you talking about *God*?"

Jeffries smirks. "Let's look at the evidence first before we make a decision." He points back to his drawing. "The first piece of evidence in Jason's mystery was simply the shoebox itself. How did it get in the attic in the first place?"

"My grandpa put it there, based on the evidence," replies Jason.

"Good," says Jeffries. "Does anyone know how the universe got here? Was it always here?"

"I don't think so," says Hannah. "My older sister Cameron is in high school, and her teacher said the universe simply *popped* into existence. She called it the 'Big Bang.' Cameron learned about it in her science class."

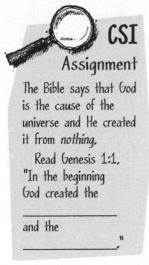

CSI Assignment

The Bible says that God is the cause of the universe and He created it from *nothing*.

Read Genesis 1:1. "In the beginning God created the

_____

and the

_____ ."

"Like the Big Bump," jokes Daniel. "We learned *that* in Jason's attic."

All the cadets laugh. "Ha!" says Jeffries. "Except with the bump, something caused it, whether the cat did it, or something else, right? As for the universe, scientists seem to think there was a Big Bang, yes. And here's something even more interesting …" Jeffries leans closer to the cadets and lowers his voice. The cadets are listening eagerly.

"These same scientists think that everything in the universe, all space, time, and matter, came into existence from *nothing*."

"Everything in the universe started from just *empty space*?" asks Jason.

"No," responds Jeffries. "Space isn't *nothing*; space is *something*. Scientists believe that before the universe existed, there wasn't even *space*. No space, no time, and no matter."

Everyone sits for a moment to think about what Detective Jeffries just said.

Jason breaks the silence. "That's kind of hard to imagine ... I mean, the idea of *nothing*."

Hannah has that expression on her face again, like she's thinking hard. "Wait a minute. So, if nothing existed before the universe ... I mean truly nothing ... what caused the universe to begin? What created it?"

" ...what caused the universe to begin?"

"What created it?"

Hannah has that expression on her face again, like she's thinking hard.

Jeffries smiles. "That's a really good question. The shoebox couldn't cause itself to exist, and the universe can't cause itself to exist either. Everything that has a beginning must be caused by something else. The cause of the shoebox couldn't be found inside the shoebox, and the cause of the universe can't be found inside the universe either."

A "Tool" for Your Detective Bag!

Take It in Order

When investigating a mystery, put first things first. Start by collecting the evidence, then figure out how the evidence got in the scene. Don't get ahead of yourself and ... be patient.

"What exists outside the universe that could cause it to pop into existence?" asks Daniel.

"Well, the more evidence we study, the better answer we'll have," says Jeffries. "We know a few things about the shoebox, for example. It wasn't in the attic *forever*, and the items in the box didn't appear in the box on their own. The best explanation for the items *inside* the box is someone *outside* the box. And finally, based on the evidence in the box, Grandpa Ren is the most reasonable explanation. Does all this make sense so far, Jason?"

"Yes sir," replies Jason.

"Now, let's turn our attention to our investigation of the universe," says Jeffries, as he adds something to his diagram.

"So far, we've only talked about one fact: We live in a universe that has a beginning. And even though we don't have a lot of evidence yet, we can start to think about a *Suspect Profile*—a picture of how the cause of the universe might be described, given the facts we have.

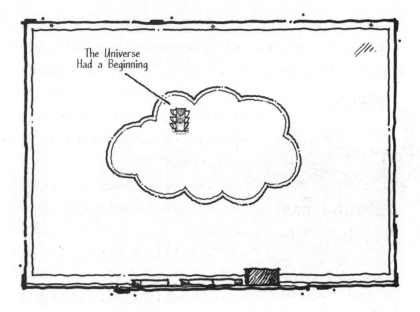

"Here's what we know about our 'suspect' so far. First, it caused the universe to come into existence. Second, it isn't made up of space, time, or matter. And third, it's powerful enough to create everything we see in the universe from nothing."

Detective Jeffries turns back to the cadets.

"Looks like we're on our way to solving two mysteries," he declares.

"A shoebox and a universe!" you say.

"I still want to know *why* Grandpa Ren put this stuff in the shoebox and what he meant in his message to me," says Jason.

"Oh, we're going to get all those answers, Jason. Don't you worry. But remember, impatience is not a good detective skill."

The cadets laugh as the session ends and they leave the briefing room.

Chapter Two

All Tuned Up

Who Is Responsible?

"Follow me to the forensics lab," commands Detective Jeffries before everyone can get seated at the next Junior Academy session. The cadets appear excited about their first chance to visit the place where science and detective investigations *collide*.

They descend a set of stairs to the bottom floor of the police department. The first room of the lab is filled with technicians sitting at their desks, studying images and files on wide computer screens. This room is separated from the next by a long wall of windows. Through the glass, you can see more technicians working in the adjacent room, studying evidence laid out on tables.

"Circle around," says Jeffries, as he guides the cadets into an examination room. This room is smaller. On one end of the room is a whiteboard and a few chairs. There's a table in the center, covered with wide white paper. The evidence bag containing the shoebox is sitting in the center of the papered surface. Jeffries puts on a light blue apron, plastic gloves for his hands, and a cap for his hair. "Let's take a closer look at this shoebox. What do you see?"

Each cadet leans in to peer at the box. "It looks worn," says one of the cadets. "Or should I say *deteriorated*?"

"What else?" encourages Jeffries.

"The tiny holes," says Daniel. "On the edge, see? They're unusual; they look like they were made by something that tried to *eat* at the edges of the box."

"Good observation. Do you see anything else?" asks Jeffries.

Hannah says, "The items *inside* the box don't appear to be worn or damaged. Look at the paper note and drawing. And I'd say it's lucky that the holes at the edges of the box weren't so big that they allowed the things inside, the ring for example, to slip out."

"Or allowed whatever caused those holes to get in!" says Jason.

"I think Hannah's observation about the *size* of the holes is important," notes Jeffries. "Was it just *luck* that these holes weren't bigger? What do you think caused them in the first place?"

Detective Definitions

Reasonable Inference:

Not everything that's *possible* is *reasonable*. Detectives look for the most reasonable explanation (also called an "inference").

The holes in the shoebox, for example, are most reasonably explained by the mice in the attic.

"I know the answer to that question," says Jason, as he steps toward the table. "We've had problems with mice in the past. That's why we originally got Simba, but even *he* couldn't keep up with them. I bet those holes were caused by mice eating away at the objects in the attic."

"I did see mousetraps up there," you recall.

Just then, a technician knocks on the door of the examination room. "Here are the photos you ordered, Detective." She hands several printed images to Jeffries.

"Thanks, Carol—just in time." Jeffries turns to the whiteboard. Using small, round magnets, he begins to post the photos on the surface of the board. They display the attic as Jeffries photographed it during the last session.

"Yes, we can see these mousetraps on the floor of the attic," says Jeffries, pointing to one of the photos.

Jason suggests, "So it wasn't really 'luck' that prevented the holes in the box from getting bigger. They stayed small because my grandma Miri got Simba and even put those traps in the attic."

"Good point," replies Jeffries. "In many ways, your grandma controlled the environment of the house and the attic to make sure its contents survived without much damage. You might say she 'fine-tuned' your home, Jason."

"What do you mean by 'fine-tuned'?" you ask.

"Well, I can think of several alternative scenarios in which the shoebox might have been completely destroyed by rodents." Detective Jeffries starts to draw on the whiteboard. "Let's say, for example, that Jason's grandparents decided to buy a house in the country instead of one here in the city. In the countryside, where things are a bit more wild, there would have been an even greater possibility of mouse and rodent damage. So even at the 'foundational' level of where Jason's home is *located*, it's not an accident that there are fewer critters to destroy things.

"Add to this the fact that Grandma Miri got a cat to help control the mice. So, from the 'regional' perspective of Jason's *house*, it's also not an accident that there is less of a rodent problem."

"Simba *is* a pretty good hunter," says Jason.

"Finally, to *make sure* there weren't any rodents in the attic, Grandma Miri set mousetraps," says Jeffries as he points to the drawing. "She intervened at what I call the 'locational' level."

"And that's why the things in the shoebox survived," says Daniel.

"That's right. It wasn't an accident. When we see this kind of intervention, this kind of 'fine-tuning' at all three of these levels, it's reasonable to conclude that someone intentionally acted to make sure the items in the attic survived."

Jeffries puts down his marker. "Now that you've learned about 'fine-tuning' and the three levels of evidence collection, let's go back to the briefing room and apply this to the universe."

"It's reasonable to conclude that someone intentionally acted to make sure the items in the attic survived."

Locational Tuning:
Traps

Regional Tuning:
Simba

Foundational Tuning:
Location

Layers of Fine-Tuning

"Remember the diagram I just drew of Jason's house?" Jeffries asks, as the cadets retake their seats in the briefing room. "Let's make a similar diagram of the entire universe." He starts drawing again on the whiteboard.

"Just as we found evidence of fine-tuning at Jason's house—in the 'foundational,' 'regional,' and 'locational' levels—we find similar levels of fine-tuning in the universe."

The cadets are trying to copy Jeffries's diagram on their notepads.

"The 'foundational' conditions of the universe are incredibly fine-tuned." Detective Jeffries turns to the cadets and holds up his marker, then drops it to the floor. You recognize this example from your first Junior Academy experience with Jeffries, but for many of the other cadets in the room, this is their first time seeing it.

"Did you notice how fast the marker fell?" Jeffries asks. Why didn't it fall faster, or slower? Why did it fall to the ground *at all*?"

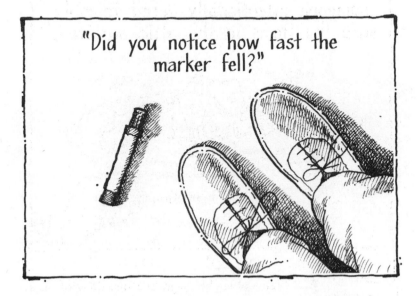

"The force of gravity caused it to fall," says one of the cadets.

"Exactly, but did you ever stop to think that the force of gravity must be *just so*—not too strong and not too weak—for our universe to exist?"

"You mean like the porridge in the story of Goldilocks and the three bears?" you say. "Gravity is *just right*?" A few of the cadets giggle.

"That's *precisely* what I mean. And it's not just gravity. All the *other* forces in the universe, and even the forces in the *atom*, have to be perfectly fine-tuned, or our universe wouldn't exist and there certainly wouldn't be any *life* in the cosmos."

"But what if these forces were just a bit stronger or just a bit weaker? We'd adjust to that, right?" asks Jason.

Jeffries shakes his head. "Actually, *no*. Scientists have discovered that the *tiniest* difference in any of the dozens of foundational forces of the universe would *prevent life altogether*.

CSI Assignment

The Bible confirms that God fine-tuned the universe so that life can exist.

Read what King David wrote in Psalm 19:1-2. "The heavens are telling of the glory of _____ ; and their expanse is declaring the work of His _____.

Why do you think God wants life to exist in the universe?

"And there's more," adds Jeffries, as he turns back to the whiteboard. "At the regional level of the galaxies and star systems, there's even *more* evidence of fine-tuning."

"Star systems? You mean like our *solar system*?" you ask.

"Yes. Our sun, and the other planets in our solar system, are perfectly fine-tuned so life can exist here on earth. The position, shape, age, and mass of our sun are *just right*, like Goldilocks's porridge. If our sun were any different, life couldn't exist on our planet."

"I never thought of our sun like *porridge*," says Daniel.

"Even our *galaxy* is like Goldilocks's porridge," adds Jeffries.

"You mean the Milky Way?" asks Hannah.

"Yes, even the Milky Way is fine-tuned for the existence of life," says Jeffries, as he draws the shape of our galaxy on the whiteboard. "Only about 5 percent of the galaxies in the universe have spiral arms like ours. If our universe were shaped differently, or larger than it is, the radiation from its core would make life impossible."

"So, our galaxy needs some 'milk' to cool it down," quips Daniel. Everyone laughs.

"Not quite," says Detective Jeffries, "but you get the idea. One more thing ..." Jeffries begins drawing again on the whiteboard. "At the 'locational' level of our home planet, Earth, conditions are *also* fine-tuned for life.

"Our planet has the right kind of sun, atmosphere, ground surface, and even the right kind of *moon* to make life possible. Just like Jason's house and the three levels of fine-tuning we observed, there are three levels of fine-tuning in the universe."

Dig Deep
Visit the Online Academy

Watch your penmanship as you complete your fill-in sheets. If you aren't neat and disciplined in your notebook, you won't be organized and disciplined as a detective!

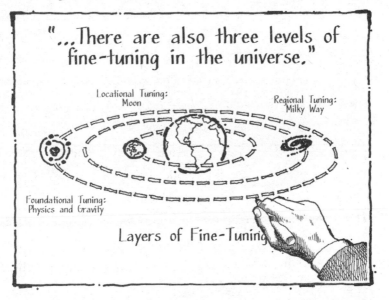

"...There are also three levels of fine-tuning in the universe."

Locational Tuning: Moon

Regional Tuning: Milky Way

Foundational Tuning: Physics and Gravity

Layers of Fine-Tuning

Jeffries turns from the whiteboard to the cadets with a serious look on his face. "Now think about what we investigated in our first session," he prompts.

Daniel raises his hand and says, "I remember we discovered the universe couldn't have been created from an *inside* cause. It came from 'nothing,' so it must have been caused by something outside of space, time, and matter."

"Correct. Now let's look at the three levels of fine-tuning we've discovered. Could something *inside* the universe have caused everything to be *just so?*"

"I don't know," Jason says. "Maybe there isn't any other way the universe *could be*. Isn't it possible that the universe just *had* to be this way?"

"Great question," replies Jeffries. "The answer is *no*. At least not according to our best scientists. The forces we described could have been *very* different, and so could the shape of the galaxies, star systems, and even our planet."

"We learned something interesting about the shoebox today," says Jeffries. "The items in the shoebox survived because Jason's grandparents *fine-tuned* the environment. They bought a house in the city, got Simba as a pet, and set the mousetraps."

Jeffries points to his diagram of the universe:

"Our universe seems to be similar. If the forces in the universe weren't *just so*, if our galaxies and star systems weren't *just right*, and if Earth weren't *fine-tuned* as it is, life in the universe would not have emerged and survived." Detective Jeffries adds this piece of evidence to the diagram.

The cadets think about this for a moment. Hannah says, in a hushed tone, "If the fine-tuning we saw at Jason's house is evidence that Grandma Miri was involved as a fine-tuner, does that mean the fine-tuning we see in the universe is evidence of some kind of powerful fine-tuner? It seems like somebody's working the controls, or none of us would be here."

A "Tool" for Your

Detective Bag!
Look for Layers

When collecting evidence to solve a mystery, organize your evidence by *layers* (if possible). The more layers you have, the better your conclusions.

Everyone is quiet for a minute.

Then Jeffries says, "I do think we can add something to our *Suspect Profile* from the last session." He reminds the cadets of the profile he began last week. "Whatever *caused* the universe also fine-tuned it with a *purpose in mind*—the existence of life."

"A *purpose?*" you ask.

"Yes, our universe appears to have been fine-tuned so life like ours could exist." Jeffries puts down his marker.

The cadets are quietly thinking about everything they've learned.

"Next time we'll take a closer look at the *contents* of the shoebox so we can figure out what *Grandpa Ren's* purpose was when he wrote the letter," says Jeffries.

"Finally!" blurts out Daniel, impatiently.

Everyone laughs as this week's session comes to a close.

Chapter Three

Directions for Life

Does the Text Require an Author?

Detective Jeffries is standing at the front of the briefing room, opening the evidence bag that contains the shoebox. He's covered one of the tables with white paper, and he's wearing his gloves and blue apron.

"Let's all gather around the evidence," he says, as he removes the items from the box.

Jeffries picks up the drawing of a boy standing next to a tree and asks, "Did any of you notice that of all the items in the box, two contain *information*?"

Jason raises his hand. "The note from my grandpa was *written* to me ..." he says.

"Yes, and this drawing *also* contains information," adds Jeffries. "The other items can be investigated for their meaning, but these two objects, the note and the drawing, are an obvious attempt by someone to *tell* us something."

"I never thought of a *drawing* that way before," says one of the cadets.

"Artists are communicators, just like authors," says Detective Jeffries, as he uses magnets to post the drawing on the whiteboard so everyone can see it. "Let's try to figure out what the artist is trying to tell us."

Everyone looks at the drawing. A boy with black hair is standing under an unusual tree with delicate red leaves.

Jason seems to be concentrating. "I bet that's the tree in my backyard!" The other cadets lean in closer. "There's a tree planted in our yard, and it's the only one with red leaves."

Someone says, "So, is the boy in the drawing *you*, Jason?" The cadets look intently from the drawing to Jason and back again. Jason starts to feel a bit awkward, but eventually admits, "I guess it could be me …"

"Grab your notepads," commands Detective Jeffries. "I think it's time for another field trip."

CSI Assignment

God wants you to ask questions so you can be certain that He exists and the Bible is true.

Read James 1:5. "But if any of you lacks wisdom, let him who gives to all generously and without reproach, and it will be given to him."

Have you been talking to God and asking Him your questions?

The cadets take the short walk around the corner to Jason's house, talking loudly among themselves and speculating about the meaning of the drawing. They gather at the gate that opens into Grandma Miri's backyard and garden.

"Back again so soon?" asks Grandma Miri, as she opens the gate. She's smiling again from ear to ear. "I could hear you coming from around the corner!"

Jason explains everything to his grandmother as she welcomes the cadets into the backyard. They circle around the tree with the delicate red leaves.

It is very large and surrounded by a beautiful flower bed.

"It definitely looks like the tree in the drawing," you say, as Detective Jeffries joins the group.

"Yes, it does," he agrees. Let's use this opportunity to develop another detective skill."

They circle around the tree with the delicate red leaves.

The cadets pull out their notepads and get ready to write.

"Every investigation involves answering key questions," begins Jeffries, "and some questions are more important than others. Detectives focus on the 'five Ws and the one H.'"

The cadets have expressions on their faces like they aren't quite sure what he means.

"In every investigation," he continues, "we must remember to ask the *what, why, when, where, how,* and *who* questions."

"My English teacher makes us answer those questions in our essays," one of the cadets remarks.

"Your teacher would be a good detective," says Jeffries. As the cadets are getting comfortable sitting on the grass around the tree, Simba appears from the side of the house and joins them. The cat immediately jumps into Hannah's lap and pushes his face under her chin.

"Sorry about Simba," Grandma Miri says. "He loves people and loves being petted. And he's not bashful about asking!"

Hannah giggles and begins to scratch Simba's head.

"Grandma Miri, can we ask you a few questions about this tree?" inquires Detective Jeffries. She nods in agreement.

Before Jeffries can begin, the cadets respond to a noise in the next yard. They look toward the edge of the garden and see a curious face peering over the top of the neighbor's fence.

Detective Definitions

Interview:

Detectives conduct interviews of witnesses and experts to gather information. This information is then used to find the truth and share it with others.

Good detectives are curious; when interviewing others, they ask specific questions based on their curiosity.

If you want to be a good interviewer, you have to start with good questions. Be specific and thorough.

"Hi, Jasmine," says Jason. "Everybody, meet Jasmine, our neighbor. Come on over and we'll explain what's going on."

Jasmine *jumps over* the fence to join them.

To everyone's surprise, Jasmine *jumps over* the fence to join them. Jason describes the mystery to her, and when he's finished, Jeffries begins with his first question.

"I want to start with a *what* question," he says. "What kind of tree is this?"

"It's called a *Bloodgood* tree," says Grandma Miri, as she rubs the trunk of the large tree and looks up at its branches.

"That sounds like the kind of tree a detective would investigate!" says Daniel, trying to get a laugh from the other cadets.

"Perhaps it does," responds Grandma Miri, "but it really has more to do with the color of the leaves." Everyone looks up at the red leafy canopy overhead.

"Is that a nest?" asks one of the cadets, pointing to a cluster of twigs on one of the lower branches.

Before anyone can respond, Jasmine jumps up and starts *climbing the tree*. "I'll check!" Within seconds she reports, "It looks abandoned. Can I keep it?" Grandma Miri smiles and nods. Jasmine climbs down and nearly trips on something sticking up in the flower bed at the base of the tree. She stumbles, blushes for an instant, then sits back down with the other cadets as she holds the empty nest.

Before anyone can respond, Jasmine jumps up and starts climbing the tree.

"Now I've got a *where* question for you," says Jeffries, returning to his interview. "I've never seen another tree like this, and I've lived in this area my entire life. Where did it come from?"

"Japan," Grandma Miri answers. Many of the cadets are surprised by her answer.

"Japan?" asks Jeffries. "Wow, I guess I better ask a *how* question. How did this tree get here from Japan?"

"My husband Ren's family had a nursery in Japan. They raised many kinds of plants and trees, including Japanese maple trees. This Bloodgood tree is one of many maple trees they used to grow. Ren's father sent us seeds to grow it here in America."

CSI Assignment

Jesus was a good interviewer, even when He was very young.

Read Luke 2:41-46.

"After three days they found Him in the temple, sitting in the midst of the teachers, both _____ to them and asking them _____."

Jeffries pauses. "Hmm. I've asked *what*, *where*, and *how* questions; can I ask a *why* question now? Why did you want this kind of tree in your yard?"

Grandma Miri smiles and looks affectionately at Jason. "Ren wanted to plant this special tree to commemorate the birth of Jason. He was our first grandchild. Ren wanted Jason to grow up with a tree that meant a lot to Ren's family."

"Cadets," says Detective Jeffries, "we've asked four of our six detective questions, and along the way we've gotten answers we didn't expect related to *when* and *why* the tree was planted. For example, *when* was this tree planted in the yard?"

"When Jason was born, to celebrate his birth," you answer.

"That's correct. And *who* planted the tree?"

"Grandpa Ren," says Jasmine. She's still holding the nest and doing her best to fend off Simba, who's taken an interest in her find.

"And, oh, you should have been here to see how careful my Ren was when he planted this tree," says Grandma Miri, shooing Simba from Jasmine's lap.

"What do you mean, Grandma Miri?" asks Jeffries.

"Ren got the seeds in the mail from his father. They came with very specific instructions about how to plant and nurture them until we had a maple *sapling*. They had to be fertilized *just so*, and the young tree had to be moved from the sapling pot to the ground in a very specific way. Ren followed his father's instructions *to the letter* to make sure the tree would survive." Grandma Miri gazes up at the broad branches and delicate leaves. "And look at it now …"

Jeffries thanks Grandma Miri and directs the cadets to return to the police station. "You may not realize it, but you just learned something important we can apply to our investigation of the *universe*."

Detective Definitions

Key Interview Questions:

Of all the questions a detective must ask, the *who* question is the most important.

You might learn a lot about a crime scene by asking the *what*, *where*, and *how* questions, but only the *who* question will lead you to the suspect who committed the crime.

"We've investigated two important attributes of the universe," reminds Jeffries, as all the cadets take their seats back in the briefing room. "Who can recall what we've examined so far?"

"The universe has a beginning … and the universe is fine-tuned for life," you offer.

"Exactly," says Jeffries. "Now I want to offer a third piece of evidence: life in our universe appeared from non-life." Jeffries modifies one of his earlier drawings to include this fact.

"Life from non-life?" asks Jason.

"Yes, all the living creatures in our universe; everything on our planet from bacteria, to simple cellular organisms, to plants like Jason's maple tree, to animals like Simba and even humans like all of us in this room—these living things came from *non-living matter*. Think about that for a minute."

Jason asks, "Do scientists know how this happened?"

"No," says Jeffries. "They've tried many explanations, but none really seem to answer that question." Detective Jeffries writes the six detective questions on the whiteboard. "Every time they ask one of these important detective questions, they fail to get a satisfying answer. In fact, some of these questions just lead to additional, *more difficult* questions."

Jeffries lifts his marker to the whiteboard. "When it comes to the *what* question, scientists are only now beginning to understand that living organisms are *very* complex. Life is not simple, and it didn't begin easily in the universe." Jeffries draws a line through the *what* question on the whiteboard.

"My sister's science teacher said life began in the ocean," remarks Daniel.

"That brings us to the *where* question," adds Jeffries, as he turns again to the whiteboard. "Scientists have investigated several places as they try to figure out where all the right ingredients could come together to bring things to life. No matter where they look, they can't find a place where the right ingredients for life could be assembled in just the right way." He draws a line through the *where* question.

"It doesn't sound like we have a lot of answers," says Hannah quietly.

"You're right, Hannah. When it comes to the *what, where, when,* and *why* questions, scientists don't have good answers and they don't often agree on the few answers they *do* have."

"Are there any questions that scientist *can* answer?" asks Jason.

Jeffries smiles and begins to draw something on the whiteboard. "Yes. In fact, we've learned something about life that is *really* interesting. We've discovered something called *DNA*.

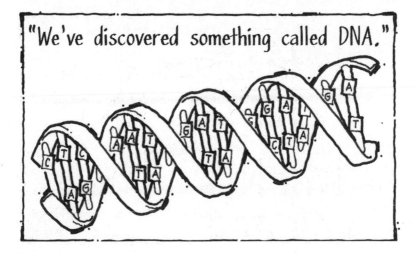

"In your body, DNA molecules carry the full 'map' for everything about you, from your eye color to the way your body heals itself when it gets sick. Your DNA contains all the information needed for you to be who you are. There's enough information in your DNA to fill a million-page book."

Detective Definitions

Information:

Knowledge that is sent so it can be understood by those who receive it.

Information requires an intelligent source because the sender must make intelligent choices between the words, letters, or images he or she is using.

When detectives see information, they know an intelligent suspect has been there.

"Whoa," says Daniel, looking at his stomach. "All *that's* in *here* somewhere?"

Jeffries laughs, "It's all very small, at the *molecular* level."

"Who wrote that information?" asks Hannah.

"Why did you ask that, Hannah?" replies Jeffries.

"Well, you said DNA contains information, so I was wondering who wrote the information …" Hannah looks like she really wants an answer.

Detective Jeffries circles the *who* question on the whiteboard. "It's interesting that you thought the author of the DNA information was a *who*." Jeffries turns to the cadets. "Do you remember the instructions that Grandpa Ren had to follow to make sure the tree would grow and survive?"

The cadets nod as they remember the story from Grandma Miri.

"When Grandpa Ren got that note from his father, he knew an intelligent being—a *who* (his dad)—had written it. He knew information didn't get on that note by *accident*. Only *intelligent persons* can write information like the kind Ren saw on those instructions."

Jeffries points to the DNA diagram on the whiteboard. "The information in DNA is far more complicated than the information on Grandpa Ren's note from his dad. If we know *that* note came from an intelligent *who*, why wouldn't we believe the information in DNA came from an intelligent *who*?" He lifts his marker and adds a third piece of evidence to the diagram of the universe:

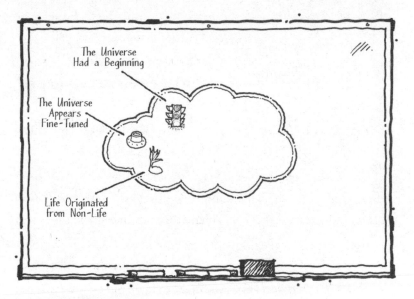

"What kind of *who* could write the information in DNA?" asks Jason.

"Detective Jeffries, are you talking about *God* again?" asks Hannah. "A Creator seems like the one possibility that makes sense."

"First, let's review what we've learned about the shoebox," says Jeffries. "The drawing appears to show the tree in Jason's backyard, and the boy in the drawing might be Jason. Also, the person who drew the picture wants viewers to focus their attention on the tree for some reason."

"I still have lots of questions about the letter in the shoebox, though ..." starts Daniel.

"I do too, but—" answers Jeffries.

"I know, I know," says Daniel. "Good detectives are patient." Everyone laughs.

"Our *Suspect Profile* is growing," says Jeffries after the cadets settle down.

"Whatever caused the universe to come into existence from nothing and fine-tuned it for life was also *intelligent and able to communicate*—as we saw in our DNA."

"Our 'suspect' is starting to sound a lot like God," says Hannah.

Jeffries smiles, "We're not done yet, and remember ..."

"Good detectives are patient!" says Daniel, as he looks around the room and waits for everyone to respond.

You and Jason start laughing as Jeffries dismisses the group for another week.

Chapter Four

The Obvious Artist

Is There Evidence of an Artist?

This week's Academy Session begins in the forensics lab. Several pairs of magnifying glasses are lying on the papered table, along with a variety of short and long tweezers. There's also a box of latex examination gloves. Detective Jeffries is the last to enter the room.

"I'm glad you're all here," he says, as he puts the evidence bag on the table and starts taking out everything from the shoebox. "I want everyone to glove up and grab a magnifying glass."

The cadets respond by quickly putting on their latex gloves.

"Okay," says Jeffries, "it's time for each of you to exercise your detective thinking skills. Start by passing around the items we discovered in the box. Handle them carefully. If you need to, you can use the tweezers and magnifying glasses to examine them."

The cadets begin to pass the objects to one another. Some use the tweezers to examine Ren's letter and the drawing. Others simply hold the shovel and other objects with their gloved hands. You and Jason carefully study the outside of the ring with your magnifying glasses. On one side of the ring are the letters *GGS* engraved into it.

"I have an important question for you," says Jeffries. All the cadets stop what they're doing and look up. "Look carefully at all the objects and even the shoebox we found them in. What do these items have in common?"

"I found them in the attic?" asks Jason, tentatively.

"Well, that's true, but I have something else in mind," responds Jeffries, as he reaches into his pocket. "Maybe this will help …"

He pulls out a small rock and puts it on the table.

"Compare the items you found in the attic to the rock," says Jeffries. "How are they *different*?"

The students talk with one another, then Daniel jokes, "We didn't find the rock in the attic!" Several cadets laugh as Daniel smiles proudly.

"That's not exactly what I had in mind either," replies Jeffries. "Anyone else?"

Jason cautiously raises his hand, "I think I might know … The rock wasn't created by a *human*, but all the other items *were*."

"Exactly," says Jeffries. "The shoebox and the items inside were crafted by *intelligent beings*. They're *designed*, but the rock is just the result of accidental, natural events."

"That seems obvious, now that you mention it," says Hannah.

"But *why* is it obvious?" asks Detective Jeffries.

"You can just *tell*!" says one of the cadets.

At that moment, the door to the examination room opens and one of the lab technicians escorts Jasmine into the room. She's carefully carrying the bird's nest she retrieved from Jason's tree.

She's carefully carrying the bird's nest she retrieved from Jason's tree.

"Jasmine, what are *you* doing here?" asks Jason.

"I invited her," explains Jeffries.

"Hi, everyone!" says Jasmine. She appears to be a bit in awe as she looks around the high-tech room and sees that everyone is wearing examination gloves.

"I asked Jasmine to bring the nest for a reason," continues Jeffries. "Be very careful now, and examine the nest as you did the other objects."

The cadets slowly pass the nest to one another, each using his or her magnifying glass and tweezers to examine its construction.

"Okay, tell me about the nest," Jeffries says, as he begins to draw a diagram on the examination room whiteboard. "Is the nest more like the items in the shoebox, or more like the rock?"

"Like the items in the box," you say. "It looks like it was designed."

"It wasn't just the result of accidental, natural events?" asks Detective Jeffries.

"No," says Daniel. "Birds obviously built it."

"Fine, but I want you to think like *detectives*," says Jeffries. "What *evidence* do you have that this nest was intelligently designed by birds? Let's make a list."

Hannah raises her hand. "Well, how about this? It doesn't seem likely that these twigs could come together in this way by *accident*."

Detective Definitions

Artifacts:

An *artifact* is a *designed object* that shows the workmanship of an intelligent *artisan*.

When detectives find an artifact at the scene of an investigation, they know it has been made or placed there by an intelligent being (usually a human, and hopefully their suspect!).

Artifacts show evidence of design.

"Good," says Jeffries, as he writes this on the whiteboard. "What else?"

"It looks like other things we know were designed," observes Daniel, "like a bowl made by a potter."

"That's a great observation," commends Detective Jeffries. "If we know that bowls are designed objects, why wouldn't we think the nest is designed?" Jeffries adds this to his growing list on the whiteboard.

Daniel is holding the nest very close to his face, looking at it with a magnifying glass. "Did you all notice how the twigs aren't just lying together randomly? They're actually woven together a little bit so they stay together as a nest."

"Can I add something?" asks Jasmine.

"Of course," replies Jeffries, as he hands the nest to her.

"I've had some time to study the nest at home, and I was amazed that the birds seemed to have a *goal*. They put larger, stiffer twigs on the outside of the nest to build it nice and strong, but used finer, softer pine needles on the inside to make it soft enough to hold eggs. It's as if the birds' purpose, from the very beginning, was to build a house with a soft bed." The cadets stand in silence. They are impressed with Jasmine's observation.

"Wow," says Hannah. "Jasmine's a pretty good detective—and she hasn't even been part of the Academy!"

Jeffries laughs and adds this observation to the list of evidence.

"Couldn't gravity have caused some of these twigs to fall into place, though?" asks Jason.

"Maybe," replies Jeffries, "but do you think this nest could come together, as we see it today, just because of gravity or some law of nature?"

Jason thinks about it. "No, I don't think so."

"Let's add that fact to our list," says Jeffries, as he turns again to the whiteboard.

"Okay, take a look at what we have so far, everyone. I've drawn the nest and five good pieces of evidence that indicate it was created by intelligent birds—it didn't just fall into place by accident or through some natural law."

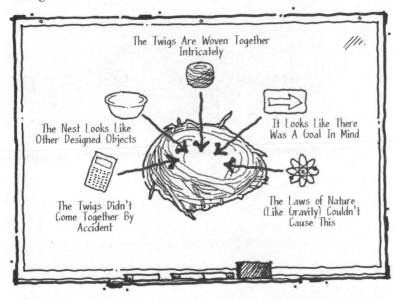

Jeffries turns his attention to Jasmine. "You said you were amazed by what you saw in this little nest …" He then looks toward the cadets. "I think you'll all be *more* amazed at what you're about to see in something much smaller. Let's go up to the briefing room."

 Detective Jeffries immediately starts drawing on the whiteboard upstairs. Everyone looks intently at the elaborate and detailed object he is sketching. By the time he is done, the cadets are impressed.

"Wow, you're a good artist," says one of the cadets.

"Thanks," says Jeffries. He points to the object he's drawn. "This is a motor that spins a long, rope-like arm. The motor is driven by an electrical charge that causes this rotor to turn. So, tell me: Is this a product of intelligent design, or just the result of accidental, natural events?"

Almost in unison, the cadets shout, "Design!"

"Tell it to me like *detectives*," says Jeffries. "Give me some *evidence*. Think about the evidence you discovered with the bird's nest."

"Your motor is too complicated to have come together by accident," says one of the cadets.

"Good," congratulates Jeffries. "What else?"

"It looks just like the rotary engine on my dad's fishing boat," says Daniel, "and I know that was designed by a motor company."

"Fine, let's add that," says Jeffries, as he continues to write on the whiteboard.

"Everything also seems interconnected and intricate—much more than the bird's nest," you say.

"I agree," says Jeffries.

"And the motor seems designed to spin that rope-like arm. It has a purpose," adds Jasmine.

> **CSI Assignment**
>
> The Bible describes God as an intelligent designer who designed every part of our bodies, including the micro-machines in our bodies.
>
> Read Psalm 139:14. "I will give thanks to You [God], for I am _____ and _____ made; wonderful are Your _____."

"Just like your observation of the bird's nest," remembers Jeffries.

"And I guess there's no way all those motor pieces could have come together because of gravity or some other natural law," says Jason.

"You're right about that too, Jason," says Jeffries, as he finishes his diagram. "I want to tell you something about this motor, cadets."

Detective Jeffries pauses for dramatic effect. "This motor is much smaller than the nest. I just drew it large so you could see it. In fact, this motor is so small it can only be seen through a *microscope*."

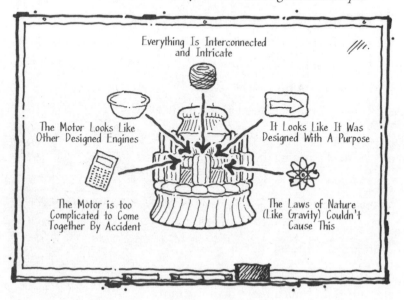

The cadets look at one another, then back at the diagram.

"It's a *bacterial flagellum*," says Jeffries, "and it's microscopic in size. This little motor isn't used to propel a *boat*; it's used by *bacteria* so they can move around."

"Wow," says Jasmine, "that *is* more amazing than my nest."

"There are thousands of other micro-machines that are just as remarkable in your body," replies Detective Jeffries, "and scientists are discovering more and more every day."

Jeffries returns to his prior diagram of the universe. "These machines are actually a fourth piece of evidence in the universe: the appearance of design in biology." Jeffries adds the fourth fact to the diagram.

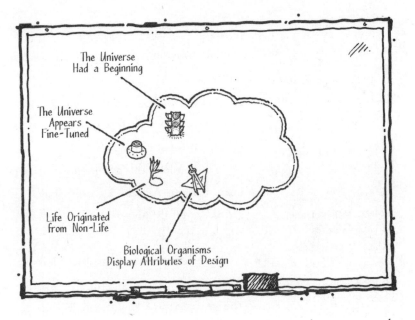

"And just like the nest," adds Jeffries, "you cadets gave me the same good evidence to indicate that micro-machines in our bodies were designed by an intelligent being."

"Wait a minute," says Jason. "How could these machines in our bodies be *designed*? Who would be the *designer*?"

"I keep saying it—we're talking about God again, right?!" Hannah says impatiently. "Who else could be the intelligent designer who could create these machines?"

"Hold on, hold on. Remember ..." starts Jeffries.

"It's important to be patient!" finishes Daniel. "At least it's not *me* this time!"

As the cadets laugh, Jeffries calls their attention to another important aspect of the growing *Suspect Profile*. "We now know something more about whatever it was that caused the universe to come into existence: Not only is it intelligent and able to communicate; it's also

A "Tool" for Your Detective Bag!
Make "Cumulative" Cases

Be sure to *accumulate* (collect) as much evidence as possible before coming to a conclusion. "Cumulative" cases (based on more than one piece of evidence) are the most reasonable and reliable.

a creative *designer*. That's why we see the obvious signs of design in the world around us."

"That's a lot to think about," you say, as you copy Detective Jeffries's diagrams into your notepad.

"I wonder if this is what my grandpa meant when he said I would 'have to think carefully about the clues,'" says Jason.

"Perhaps," says Detective Jeffries. "We've only just begun to explore the mysteries of the shoebox and the universe."

Chapter Five

Thinking about Thinking

Are We More Than Matter?

It's almost time for the next Academy Session to begin, and Detective Jeffries is standing at the front of the briefing room, checking his watch and walking back and forth near the whiteboard.

"*Now* look who's impatient," whispers Daniel to Jason.

"I heard that!" says Jeffries in a booming voice. "I know some of you have been eager to figure out what Grandpa Ren meant when he wrote in his note to 'think carefully about the clues.'"

Many of the cadets nod in agreement.

"Today we are going on a field trip that will help you understand what it means to *think* in the first place. Gather your things and join me as we walk down the street to the coroner's office. We have an appointment there in a few minutes."

The coroner's office? Why is Detective Jeffries taking us there, you wonder, as you walk briskly with the other cadets. The office looks professional on the outside, a little like a hospital. In the lobby, Detective Jeffries talks to the receptionist. Moments later, a woman wearing a white lab coat enters and greets Jeffries and the cadets.

"This is Dr. Jennifer Kelley, cadets," says Jeffries. Dr. Kelley smiles warmly and waves hello. "She'll be giving us a brief tour of the coroner's office.

Some of the cadets whisper with one another. Many still wonder how any of this is related to Grandpa Ren's note or the shoebox.

"Let's begin," says Dr. Kelley, as she opens the door to a long hallway. "I am a deputy coroner here and I sometimes get to help people like Detective Jeffries investigate suspicious deaths."

Some of the cadets already have questions. Daniel raises his hand. "You said you're a deputy; are you in law enforcement?"

"No," responds Dr. Kelley, as she guides everyone down the hallway. "I'm a licensed doctor, just like the kind of doctor you visit when you are sick, only I have a specialty: *dead people*."

Hannah stops in her tracks. "Did you say *dead people*?"

Hannah stops in her tracks.

"Did you say dead people?"

"Yes," continues the doctor. "When someone dies suspiciously and the authorities aren't sure if it's a murder, accident, or a natural death, we examine the body to help them figure it out." The doctor stops everyone at the entrance to a large room. Two shiny metal doors push open easily from the center. "We do our examinations in this room," she says, as she invites everyone inside.

Some of the cadets are hesitant to enter. "Are dead people in there?" asks someone from the back of the group.

"No, don't worry. I'm taking you into an *empty* examination room."

The cadets enter the room and are immediately mesmerized by all the medical equipment. There are several long metal tables. Each has a large light and magnifying glass suspended by a mechanical arm. Next to the tables are large sinks and a variety of sterilized glass containers. You can see several scalpels and cutting instruments on the racks next to the tables.

"Is that what I *think* it is?" asks Daniel with an odd tone in his voice.

Dig Deep
Visit the Online Academy

Are you keeping up with the Fill-in and Activity Sheets at the God's Crime Scene for Kids Special Investigation Academy? Don't fall behind as you prepare and assemble your Academy Notebook!

He's pointing to one of the shelves next to the first sink. There's a large glass jar. Inside the container, floating in clear liquid, is a *brain*.

"It's a human brain, if that's what you mean," says Dr. Kelley. "When someone dies, we examine *every* part of their body—even their brain." She walks over and casually picks up the jar from the shelf. "This brain was donated by a family to help us study other deaths in the future."

A few of the cadets are surprised at how calmly the doctor handles something so ... gruesome.

"Cadets, this is why I brought you here," says Jeffries. "Today Dr. Kelley is going to teach us something important related to Grandpa Ren's note."

Dr. Kelley guides the group to a meeting room down the hall. After everyone is seated, she places the jar on a table next to a large whiteboard.

"Grandpa Ren's note," begins Detective Jeffries, "instructs Jason to *think* about the clues carefully. What do detectives use when they think about evidence?"

Jason points to the jar on the table. "Our brains?"

Dr. Kelley speaks up. "Do we use our brains, or do we use our *minds*?"

"What's the difference?" asks Jason.

"I'm glad you asked, Jason," replies Jeffries. "Detective work, as you know from what I taught you in our first Academy, requires us to learn how to *think*. I brought you here today to learn the difference between our *brains* and *minds* so you can understand what we are using *when* we think."

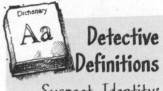

Detective Definitions

Suspect Identity:

How do detectives know the suspect being investigated is identical to the person who committed the crime?

Sometimes we ask a witness to describe the criminal they saw commit the crime. If their description is *very different* from the person we've arrested, we have good reason to believe we've got the wrong suspect!

In a similar way, if the description of the *brain* is *very different* from the description of the *mind*, we have good reason to believe they are not the same.

Jeffries turns to Dr. Kelley. "Doctor, is there a difference between the brain and the mind?"

"Yes, there are several important differences," she says, as she picks up a black marker. She draws two images and writes two headings with the words: "Brain" and "Mind."

"Sometimes people mistakenly believe your brain is the same thing as your mind, but it's not. For example, you can hold a brain in your hands. You can even put it in a jar!" Dr. Kelley holds up the glass container. "But you can't hold your mind. It's not physical or material like your brain. That's an important difference."

Dr. Kelley writes some words under the two category headings. "And you can measure this brain. You can determine how long and wide it is and how much it weighs."

"But you can't use a scale to *weigh* what I'm thinking right now," adds Daniel.

"Exactly," says the doctor, as she adds more words to the categories. "Brains are *measurable*, but minds are not."

"This brain is available for everyone to see."

"Also," says Dr. Kelley in a more serious tone, "this brain is available for everyone to see. When a person is alive, we can only see his or her brain if we perform a surgery. But even if we did that, we could never see his or her *mind*."

"That's why when someone says they're '*reading your mind*,' you know they must be joking," says Jeffries. "You can only read things you can see *publicly*, and we can't see your mind or your thoughts because you hold them *privately*."

"That's right," says the doctor. "We've just described three important reasons why we know our brains are *not* our minds." Dr. Kelley points to her list on the whiteboard. "Philosophers and scientists think there are many other ways that the brain is different than the mind, but I think these three reasons are enough for us to get the point." She lifts the jar again. "This jar contains a brain, but it doesn't contain any *thoughts*. There's a difference between brains and minds."

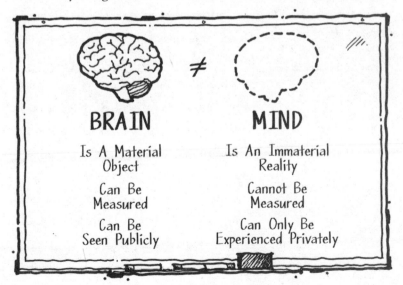

BRAIN	MIND
Is A Material Object	Is An Immaterial Reality
Can Be Measured	Cannot Be Measured
Can Be Seen Publicly	Can Only Be Experienced Privately

"So, if we're going to solve the mysteries of the shoebox and the universe, we're going to have to use our *minds*," says Detective Jeffries. "Now let's thank Dr. Kelley and use our minds to figure out how to get back to the police department."

"May I ask a question?" asks Jason, back in the briefing room. "I'm not sure why it's important to know the difference between the brain and the mind. How does any of this help us solve our cases?"

"Well," responds Jeffries, "your grandfather specifically *asked* you to *think* about the clues, and as it turns out, your *ability* to think is an important piece of evidence as we investigate the cause of the universe."

CSI Assignment

The Bible says that we are more than just physical brains and bodies.

Read 1 Thessalonians 5:23. "Now may the God of peace Himself sanctify you entirely; and may your _____ and _____ be preserved complete, without blame at the coming of our Lord Jesus Christ.

What aspects of our being are immaterial?

_____

Jeffries returns to the whiteboard. "Many scientists believe everything in the universe is made up of only space, time, and matter—and that everything can be measured, seen, or held. If that's true, we have brains but not minds, because our minds and thoughts can't be examined in any of those ways."

"But I *know* I have a mind with thoughts," declares Daniel, "because I'm *thinking* about what you just said!" Jason laughs along with some of the other cadets.

"Good point," says Jeffries. "Your common sense, and even our common experience, tells us that we do, indeed, have minds. But scientists who believe that everything *in the universe* must be explained with only what's available *in the universe*— only space, time, and matter—still aren't able to explain the existence of the *immaterial* mind."

"What if our minds came from something other than what's *inside* the universe?" you ask.

"You mean like God?" asks Hannah. Before anyone can respond to her question, she adds, "If God has thoughts and created us to be like Him, we would also have minds and thoughts, right?"

"Let's add this new piece of evidence to our diagram," says Jeffries, as he starts to draw on the whiteboard. "The existence of minds in the universe.

"This evidence allows us to add one more description to our *Suspect Profile*. Whatever caused the universe to come into existence appears to be a *mind* capable of creating *other minds*."

"I've never thought about these kinds of things before," says Daniel, "but I've heard some of my friends say, 'Seeing is believing.' They don't believe in God or angels because they say they can't see

A "Tool" for Your **Detective Bag!**
Compare Explanations

There is *always* more than one way to explain a set of facts or evidences. Be sure to list all the possible explanations and compare them to one another and to the evidence you've collected.

Is one of these explanations more reasonable than the others? Does one explain the evidence better than the others? That's the true explanation.

them. But they have thoughts and minds of their own that can't be seen or touched or measured in any way."

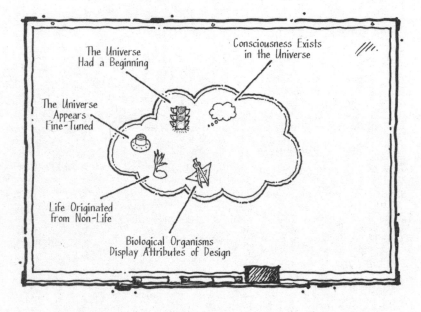

"Now maybe you can help them *think* about their *thoughts* as an example of something you can believe *without* seeing," suggests Jeffries. "There might be more to the universe than meets the eye."

Jason is thinking about the note when he says, "My grandpa said I should *think* about the clues, but he also said I would *change my mind.*" What did he want me to change my mind about?"

"We'll look at that issue *next* week …" says Jeffries with a wry smile, "… if you don't *mind.*" Some of the cadets groan and laugh as they leave the room.

"Nice pass," says Jason,
as Hannah kicks the ball
across the yard.

Chapter Six

A Change of Mind

Are Real Choices Even Possible?

"Nice pass," says Jason, as Hannah kicks the ball across the yard. He passes the ball back while they play under the broad branches of the Bloodgood tree. It's about an hour before the next Academy Session.

"Got room for one more?" asks a familiar voice from next door. Jasmine pokes her head up over the fence.

"Sure," says Jason. Grandma Miri is away running errands, but Jason knows she wouldn't mind his friends visiting in the backyard.

Jasmine climbs over the fence and turns out to be as good a soccer player as she is a fence jumper.

Their soccer session is interrupted by a loud crying noise from the tree branches. They look up and discover Simba is sitting on the very branch where Jasmine found the nest. He's crying in a strange way.

"I wonder if Simba is the reason why the bird's nest was empty," says Hannah with a smirk on her face.

"I hope not," replies Jason. "Although he is a good hunter."

"Why is he making that sound?" asks Jasmine.

"I've heard him do that before." Jason walks to the tree and stands just beyond the flower bed. "He seems to have more difficulty *coming down* from trees than he has *going up*."

"He's stuck up there?" asks Hannah.

"Probably …" Before Jason can say anything else, Jasmine starts climbing the tree.

"I'll get him," she says, and in less than a minute, she's on her way back down, carrying Simba under her right arm like a stuffed animal.

"Be careful," says Hannah, recalling that Jasmine almost tripped when she came down the tree before. "You stumbled here in the flower bed last time." She looks down and sees the edge of something sticking up out of the dirt. Jasmine is now standing at her side.

"Is that what you stumbled on last time?" Hannah asks. Simba meows. "I guess so," says Jasmine.

Jason spreads the flowers...

Jason spreads the flowers a bit to get a better look. "It's a metal box of some kind." He brushes away the dirt, but most of the box is buried and won't budge.

The cadets look at each other. "Are you thinking what I'm thinking?" says Jason to Hannah. She smiles knowingly.

"What?" asks Jasmine, as she sets Simba down on the grass.

"Well, my grandpa drew a picture of me standing next to this tree. Why? Maybe he wanted me to come here to find something."

"And in his note, he said you would have to 'dig around,'" adds Hannah.

"And he included a hand shovel!" says Jason.

"We should dig this up … right now!" exclaims Jasmine.

Everyone gets on their hands and knees and starts to dig. A strange look suddenly comes over Hannah's face. "Stop!" she yells.

"Why?" asks Jasmine.

"We can't just dig up Grandma Miri's flower bed." Hannah looks at Jason. "I mean, not until we at least get her permission."

"I agree, I guess," admits Jason.

"But we already decided as a group!" complains Jasmine. "My cousin says it's sometimes better to ask for forgiveness afterwards than permission beforehand."

Hannah laughs. "That's a funny way to put it, but this box looks like it has been buried here a long time. I guess it can stay a little longer … until we ask Grandma Miri."

"But she's not home right now," reveals Jason, as he stands back up, "and it's almost time for the Academy to start …"

They're disappointed and anxious to dig up their new discovery, but they reluctantly decide to leave the box and begin walking to the police department.

Detective Definitions

Criminal Accountability:

We *don't* blame the dominoes for falling over, but we *do* blame a sibling if he or she pushes them over. Why? Because the dominoes had no choice, but our sibling *did*.

Unless we have the true ability to make free choices, no one could be held accountable for their actions.

If our actions are simply uncontrollable physical events in our brains, no criminal could ever be blamed for a crime.

"Wow," says Detective Jeffries, "that's a fantastic discovery." He pulls the original shoebox from the evidence bag and places it on the table in the briefing room, as Jason and Hannah finish telling everyone about the buried metal box.

"Why didn't you bring it with you?" asks Daniel.

"We originally planned to dig it up," explains Jason, "but we changed our minds because we didn't want to mess up Grandma Miri's flower bed without asking first."

"Good call," says Jeffries. "So why didn't you just ask her?"

"She wasn't home," replies Jason with a disappointed look on his face.

"That's all right," says Jeffries. "Good detectives are …"

"Patient!" responds everyone in unison.

"We'll dig up the box as soon as possible," assures Detective Jeffries. "It definitely sounds like it's related to the shoebox mystery. It would explain the hand shovel and Grandpa Ren's statement about 'digging around.'"

Jeffries pauses for a moment and looks at Jason. "But Grandpa Ren also wrote that you would 'change your mind.' I wonder how he would know that?"

"Hmm." Jason is thinking. "I'm not sure."

"Well," says Jeffries, "you may have discovered important evidence in that yard—evidence that might help us solve the mystery of the shoebox *and* the mystery of the universe."

The cadets look at one another. No one is quite sure what Jeffries is talking about.

"I understand why the evidence might be important to the shoebox case, but what evidence did they discover about the universe?" asks Daniel.

Jeffries explains, "Jason and Hannah made a decision to dig up the box, right?"

"Yes, but we changed our minds," says Hannah.

"There you go—another piece of evidence!" Jeffries adds this to the universe evidence diagram: "Humans Are Free Agents."

"You mean like secret agents?" asks Daniel. "Is that why this is called a Special Investigation Academy?"

"Not exactly," says Jeffries. "All of us in this room can change our minds, just like Jason, Hannah, and Jasmine did today, and that's an important piece of evidence that can help us identify the cause of the universe."

Jeffries then abruptly leaves the briefing room. The cadets talk among themselves and wonder what the detective is up to. Moments later he returns with a small flannel drawstring bag.

"I just came from the break room down the hall," he explains, as he opens the bag and spills the contents onto the table. "Some of our employees play dominoes during their lunch breaks." An entire set of dominoes is now scattered across the surface of the table.

An entire set of dominoes is now scattered across the surface of the table.

"Do you remember last week when we talked about the difference between brains and minds?" he asks the group. "If you recall, the biggest difference between your brain and your mind is simply the fact that your brain is a physical, material object and your mind *is not*."

"That's why we can't use a tape measure to measure our thoughts," recalls Daniel.

"That's right," says Detective Jeffries, as he begins to stand up the dominoes in a line on the table. Each domino is separated from the next by less than an inch. He's careful not to knock any of them over so the entire line will remain upright.

CSI Assignment

The Bible describes the world the way it really is, especially when it comes to our ability to make free choices.

Read Joshua 24:15. Joshua tells the Israelites to "_____ for yourselves today whom you will serve ..." and then tells them that he will choose to serve the Lord.

How could the Israelites or Joshua do this unless they had free agency?

"Like we said last week, if everything in the universe is *entirely physical*—if it's all just space, time, and matter—minds don't exist, because they *aren't* physical. People who believe everything in the universe can be explained by *staying in the universe* don't believe in non-physical minds."

"So where do they say our thoughts come from?" you ask.

Jeffries responds, "They say our thoughts are simply physical events that happen in our brains." He walks over to the light switch and turns the lights off, then on again. "They believe that physical cells in our brain, called neurons, transfer electrical impulses, from one cell to another, causing a reaction, first in our brains and then in our bodies."

"So, we're like computerized robots?" asks Daniel.

"That's what some people believe," says Jeffries, walking back to the dominoes. "But there's a problem, if that's true." He stands next to the row of dominoes and extends his finger toward the first domino. "If everything that happens in our brains is purely physical, the activity between your neurons is just like this row of dominoes." He pushes the first domino, and all the others fall in sequence.

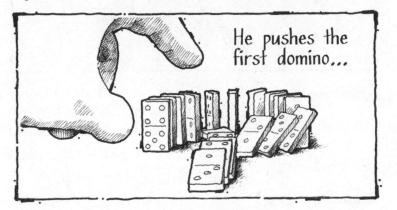

"Did you notice that once I pushed the first domino, all the others fell in order?"

All the cadets nod in agreement.

"Could any of these dominoes choose *not* to fall?" he asks.

"No," says one of the cadets.

"Why not?" Jeffries waits for an answer.

"Because they're just dominoes," says Jason. "They can't think and make their own decisions."

"Exactly," continues Jeffries. "Dominoes are just *physical objects*, so they respond without making choices. They fall because something fell against them *first*." He holds up his finger. "But did you notice that I was able to make a choice—*freely*—to start the dominoes falling?

"But, did you notice that I was able to make a choice - freely - to start the dominoes falling?"

"I didn't do it because something fell against *me* first. I just decided to do it on my own. I'm more than a *physical object*; I can act as a *free agent*."

"If the universe is only space, time, and matter," he continues, "everything in it is just a *physical object* of one kind or another, including your *brain*. And if that's the case, *you* can't make free choices any more than *dominoes* can make free choices. Every time you think, you're deciding something on your own. You're really just responding to something physical in your brain that 'fell against you first.'"

"But that's not what happened to us, today," protests Hannah. "We were going to dig up the box, but we truly *did* change our minds. We *stopped.* We thought about it, talked it over, and made a real choice. We were *in charge.*"

"It sounds like you have some firsthand evidence that the universe is more than just space, time, and matter—you have evidence that the universe *can't* be purely physical." Jeffries turns to the other cadets. "Does everyone else agree? Can you all think of times when you changed your mind or made a decision *on your own?*"

"My mom says I change my mind *too* often," says Daniel. "Especially when I'm trying to decide what flavor I want at the ice cream shop."

"My mom says I change my mind too often."

Jeffries laughs. "We all make free choices every day. But you can't get this kind of freedom unless you have something more than space, time, and matter to work with."

"God would have more to work with, wouldn't He?" asks Hannah. "He's not limited by space, time, and matter, right? If He created us to be like Him—with minds," she says, recalling their session from last week, "wouldn't this explain why we're able to think *freely*?"

"Yes," says Jeffries. "The fact that we are 'free agents' *inside the universe* tells us something about whatever caused us *outside the universe*. The cause of the universe is a *free agent* capable of creating *other free agents*."

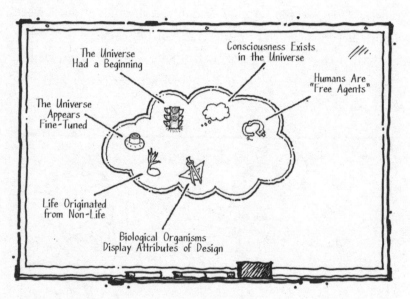

Detective Jeffries picks up the original shoebox and hands it to Jason. "The forensics lab finished photographing all these items, so I'm going to give them back to you. You might want to use that hand shovel to dig up the metal box." Jason excitedly agrees.

"Our *Suspect Profile* is almost complete," says Jeffries, "and I think we're going to solve our mysteries *very* soon. Call your parents and tell them our session will be longer today. Let's go see what's in that buried metal box."

Chapter Seven

Choosing Right from Wrong

Is Morality More Than an Opinion?

Jason is holding the shoebox tightly as he walks back home from the police department with Detective Jeffries and the other cadets. As they pass Jasmine's house, she runs up to Jason.

"Are we going to dig it up now?" she asks, her eyes bright. "I've been waiting for you guys to come home this entire time!"

"Yes," says Jason, "Detective Jeffries agrees—he thinks it might be part of the mystery."

Jason runs into his house to talk with his grandma as Detective Jeffries hands out police flashlights to some of the cadets. Moments later Jason returns.

"My grandma is on the phone right now, but she says she'll join us in a minute." Jason leads them through the backyard gate, and they gather under the Bloodgood tree.

The evening air is crisp and the sky is beginning to grow dark. One of the cadets uses a flashlight to light up the flower bed.

"There it is!" says Jasmine, as she begins to push back the flowers to expose the edge of the box.

"Don't hurt the flowers," reminds Hannah. "We said we would wait for Grandma Miri's permission, remember?"

"How much longer will she be?" asks Daniel.

"She shouldn't be long," says Jason. He can see that some of the cadets are very eager to start digging, especially now that they can see the partially buried box. He pulls the hand shovel from the shoebox.

Simba joins the group and makes his way over to the buried box.

Simba joins the group and makes his way over to the buried box. He puts a paw in the dirt, then pushes the object with his nose.

"Even Simba doesn't want to wait any longer," says Jasmine.

Jeffries is standing back, watching everything closely. "Do I need to say it?"

"Good detectives are *patient*!" shouts one of the cadets.

"It's more than that this time," says Jeffries. "You've all recognized an important moral truth while waiting for Grandma Miri. It's not okay to destroy someone's property—in this case, a flower bed—without his or her permission. I'm proud of all of you. You're choosing to do the *right thing*, even though many of you would rather just start, without asking."

Just then, Grandma Miri steps out onto the back porch and turns on the light. The yard gets a little brighter, but the cadets still need their flashlights to see the flower bed.

"Thanks for waiting for me," she says, as she approaches the cadets. "Now, what's all this fuss about my flower bed?"

Jason explains, and Grandma Miri smiles her signature smile. "I'm so glad you waited to ask me

Detective Definitions

Legal "Hierarchies":

We all recognize different levels of law we must obey. For example, there are local parking laws, state tax laws, and federal civil rights laws.

But there is an ultimate "law above all laws" at the top of the legal hierarchy: the Law of God.

about digging up my flowers. Jason knows how much I love my

garden." She looks admiringly at the entire yard, then focuses on the area under the Bloodgood tree. "Just do your best not to destroy too many of these beauties as you dig up your mystery," she says, as she scoops up Simba.

Jason and Daniel dig with the shovel and their hands. The other cadets lean over closely and do their best to light up the area with the flashlights. Only a few flowers need to be removed, and within moments, they've dislodged a small, sturdy metal box. It's worn and rusty, with a handle on its hinged top and a locking latch.

"It sure looks old," you say.

Jason brushes the dirt off the box and looks at Jeffries. "Should I open it?" he asks.

"Of course!" urges Jeffries.

Jason tries to open the latch, but it's frozen in place. He appears frustrated and starts to use his shovel to pry open the lid.

"Hold on," says Jeffries. "It's either locked, frozen shut by the rust—"

"Or both," interrupts Jason.

"Or both," agrees Jeffries. "Let's bring it back to the lab. They have what we need to unfreeze this lock, and the technicians will be there for another hour." The cadets gather their things, say good-bye to Grandma Miri, then head for the gate.

"Can I come along?" asks Jasmine.

"Sure," says Jeffries. "Just ask your parents for permission as we pass by your house."

 Back at the police station, Jeffries puts the dirty box on the clean white paper of the examination room table. "I've asked one of our techs to bring some solvent and a lockpick set. While we're waiting, I want to ask you about your decision not to destroy Grandma Miri's flower bed without her permission. Why was that the *right* thing to do?"

"Because Hannah said we should ask first," explains Jasmine.

"Is *that* what made it the right thing to do? Because Hannah said so?" asks Jeffries, looking at Jasmine. "You didn't agree with her at first, right? So why was *her* opinion about this more important than *yours*?"

"Because she's older, and bigger, than … me?" says Jasmine as she searches for a good answer.

"I think we've just discovered *another* piece of evidence in the universe: the existence of real moral truths that apply to *everyone*." Jeffries turns to the whiteboard and draws a picture of Hannah.

Jeffries turns to the whiteboard and draws a picture of Hannah.

"Most people know *right* from *wrong*, even if they don't know where these truths come from. We know that it's wrong to destroy someone's property without permission. But *how* do we know that it's wrong? Are these kinds of moral truths just a matter of *personal opinion*, like Hannah's opinion about the flower bed?"

"Maybe," says Daniel.

"Why was Hannah's opinion more important than Jasmine's?" asks Jeffries. "Was it really only because she's older and bigger?"

"No," says one of the cadets. "If that were true, all the bullies in the world would get to say what's right or wrong."

"Good point," agrees Jeffries as he draws an *X* through his sketch of Hannah. "So, we

CSI Assignment

All of us have a sense of "right and wrong," but where does this come from? According to the Bible, we know moral truth because it has been given to us by God.

Read Psalm 40:8. "I delight to do Your will, O my God; Your _____ is within my heart."

know that moral truths can't just be a matter of personal opinion. Where else might moral truths come from?"

"Well," says Daniel, as he looks at the rest of the cadets gathered in the examination room, "laws come from countries, right? So maybe moral truths come from whatever group you're part of."

"Great observation, Daniel." Jeffries does his best to draw a group of cadets above his drawing of Hannah.

"But if groups get to decide what's right and wrong, what do we do when two groups *disagree* on a moral truth?" Jeffries waits for an answer.

"We fight with each other!" exclaims Daniel. Everyone laughs.

"Don't laugh," says Jeffries, turning serious for a moment. "History is filled with examples of countries warring with one another over what they believe to be morally true."

"But if it's wrong for the biggest person—the bully—to decide what's right or wrong," says Jason, "wouldn't it also be wrong for the biggest or strongest country to decide what's right or wrong?"

Everyone quietly thinks about this.

"OK," says Jeffries as he puts another large "x" through his drawing of the group.

Jeffries breaks the silence. "Let me answer that with an imaginary scenario: If the strongest country in the world said it was okay to enslave people for the fun of it, would that make it morally right to enslave people?"

"No," says Hannah. "It's not right to have slaves, no matter what country you live in."

"Okay," says Jeffries, as he puts another large *X* through his drawing of the group. "Moral truths aren't the opinions of *people* or the opinions of *countries*. So where do moral truths come from?"

"Maybe something is morally true because everyone on the *planet* agrees," says one of the cadets.

Jeffries now draws a sketch of Earth above his drawings of Hannah and the group. "Okay, let's test that idea," he says, as he also draws a figure of a strange-looking creature on the whiteboard.

He also draws a figure of a strange looking creature.

He turns to the cadets and says, "Let's use our science fiction imaginations for a minute. Imagine we can travel in space and we discover intelligent aliens on another world." Then he points to the creature. "Would it be okay to destroy their property without asking? Do you think they would think it's okay?"

"No," says Daniel, "they probably wouldn't like it, and they look like they could *eat* us!" The cadets laugh as Jeffries puts an *X* through his drawing of Earth and the alien.

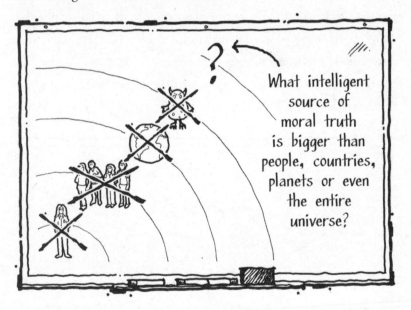

"Moral truth doesn't come from *persons*. It's bigger than that. And moral truth doesn't come from countries—or even *planets with different species*. It's bigger than these things too. So where does it come from? What intelligent source of moral truth is bigger than people, countries, planets, or even the entire universe?"

Hannah looks around the room and waits for someone else to answer. "I know," she says, finally.

"God?" asks Jason, before Hannah can finish.

"Well," she continues, "He *is* bigger than all those groups … Maybe that's why we all agree that's it's not okay to destroy things without asking—because we *all* live in a universe created by God."

"I think you're onto something," says Jeffries. He quickly sketches his diagram of the universe. "We've discovered another important piece of evidence in the universe: the existence of moral truths that apply to everyone." He adds this to his diagram. "But these truths don't come from *inside the universe*—from people, countries, or even entire planets. They come from something *bigger* than anything in the universe.

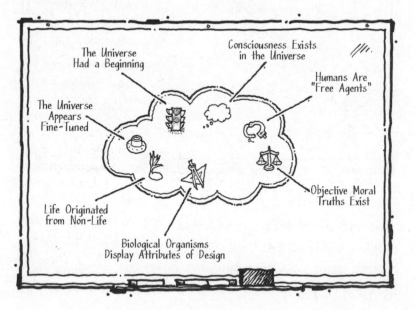

"Whatever caused the universe to come into existence from nothing, fine-tuned it for life, and designed living organisms; this cause is also the *source of all moral truth.*"

Before Detective Jeffries can say more, a lab technician knocks on the door of the examination room. She hands Jeffries the jar of solvent and the lockpick set.

The cadets gather around the table as Detective Jeffries puts on a pair of latex gloves and starts brushing the liquid solvent onto the area of the latch. The rust around the lock begins to foam and sizzle. Jeffries then opens the lockpick folder and exposes a number of wire tools, each bent slightly in a variety of thicknesses.

"Now I get to show you my *spy skills,*" he says playfully. He places one long pick in the lock of the box, then another shorter one alongside it. Jeffries carefully turns the two picks until everyone hears a metal *click.* The lid of the box pops loose.

The cadets are all wide-eyed in awe. Detective Jeffries hands the box to Jason, who opens it excitedly and reveals the contents. Inside the box is a single piece of paper. Jason takes it out, unfolds it, and reads it aloud:

A "Tool" for Your Detective Bag!
Know the Law

Detectives must memorize the law to determine if a suspect has violated it and should be arrested. You can call yourself a detective, but if you don't know the law, you're a detective *in name only.*

If you're a Christian, you also need to know and memorize God's law, unless you want to be a Christian *in name only.*

Jason, you're a good detective! I hope you enjoyed this search. Now go to my study and look in the second drawer to find your gift.

Everyone waits for Jason to say something. He begins to grin slowly, then tells the other cadets, "Let's go solve this mystery!"

Chapter Eight

Good News about Bad Things

Can God and Evil Coexist?

While racing back home, Jason tells the cadets and Detective Jeffries about Grandpa Ren's study.

"I don't go in that room very often," he says. "Grandma wants to keep it just the way Grandpa left it. She calls it her 'memory place.'"

When they arrive, Jason gathers the cadets in the living room and shows his grandma the note they found in the metal box. He gently asks her for permission to enter Ren's study.

She hesitates a moment. "It's my happiest place *and* my saddest place. Your grandpa was fifty years old when the doctor told us about his cancer." As she speaks, Simba jumps into her lap, as if to comfort her.

"For a year, he fought bravely," she says. "He was always in pain. When he was gone, I cried for days, but I was also grateful his suffering was over."

Hannah gives Grandma Miri a hug.

Detective Definitions

"Exculpatory" Evidence:

The evidence that detectives use to *prove* a suspect committed a crime is called *inculpatory* evidence, and evidence that indicates a suspect *did not* commit the crime is called *exculpatory* evidence.

Some people think pain and suffering are exculpatory evidence that disprove the existence of God, but is that true?

Jason adds, "Mom and Dad had already died in a car accident …"

Without saying anything more, Grandma Miri leads them down the hallway to Ren's study, an immaculate room filled with books and pictures. It's precisely arranged, like a monument to Ren's life.

"This desk was handed down to Ren by his father," says Grandma Miri. "He cherished it." The desk is old but beautiful, with three drawers on the right side.

Jason walks to the desk and opens the second drawer. It is empty, except for a large leather-bound Bible. Jason picks it up, and, as he does, a piece of paper falls out.

He opens the paper, then slowly reads it to the other cadets:

Jason picks up the Bible and, as he does, a piece of paper falls out.

Jason, this Bible was the Bible I used when I studied about God in seminary. I eventually earned a degree and I even served in a church for several years.

I hope you will find this Bible as valuable as I did. It is the source of all truth.

Now, use the magnifying glass and look carefully at the ring in the box. I also wanted you to have my seminary graduation ring to remind you that God is good, even in difficult times. You are part of His family. I wish I could have lived long enough to have given it to you in person. I love you, Grandpa.

"He must have written that just before he died," says Grandma Miri, smiling through her tears.

Jason takes out the magnifying glass and examines the ring with you, just as you did when you were in the forensic lab.

"I just see letters—GGS," you say.

Grandma Miri smiles and nods her head. "Golden Gate Seminary ..."

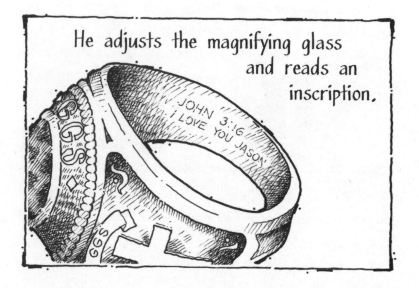

"Wait," says Jason. "There's something on the *inside* of the band."

He adjusts the magnifying glass and reads an inscription:

John 3:16. I love you, Jason.

Jason pauses for a moment. "Grandma," he asks, "why didn't you tell me Grandpa Ren was a *Christian*, or that he went to school and served in a church? Why didn't we *ever* talk about God?"

Jason's grandmother sits quietly in the chair next to the desk, looking down at her hands as she holds the letter from Ren. "When

I lost so many of the people I loved, I-I turned away from God," she says. "My faith was shattered. Ren always said that *God is love*, but I couldn't accept that anymore. I just stopped believing in God altogether."

Jason is silent.

Grandma Miri continues, "But Ren never stopped believing, even through all his pain and suffering. He was incredibly courageous and calm about it. He was convinced that God existed and that God loved him ... I wasn't so sure." She touches the ring softly. "But, I guess Ren wanted *you* to know about God so you could make up your *own* mind."

 The group is silent on the way back to the police department. The quiet continues for a moment as everyone thinks about what just happened. Detective Jeffries updates his diagrams and lists on the whiteboard.

"We've learned a lot today, haven't we?" he says, breaking the silence. Everyone agrees and begins to relax enough to start talking. Jason stands up and walks toward the diagram of the universe.

"Earlier, you said that all the evidence in the universe points to God," he says, as he looks at the diagram. "But bad things happen in the universe. The people I really care about all died before I could ever really know them. How can you believe God is real when things like this happen every day?"

Everyone stops talking. Jeffries walks over to Jason, guides him to a seat at the front table, and invites all the other cadets to circle around and sit at the table with them.

Jeffries invites all the other cadets to circle around and sit at the table with them.

"Lots of people have questioned why an all-powerful, all-loving God would allow evil to occur in the universe," says Jeffries to all the cadets. He turns to Jason. "And many people like Grandma Miri have a hard time believing in God when bad things happen to them."

Jason nods in agreement.

"But if there's more to life than just what happens to us here in the universe, it might explain why God allows things to happen to us—even *bad* things."

Jeffries asks Jason for Grandpa Ren's Bible, and opens it to the gospel of John. "Let's read that passage your grandpa engraved on the inside of his ring, John 3:16 …"

Dig Deep
Visit the Online Academy

The Academy Fill-in and Activity Sheets will help you master (and remember) the evidence. Compare each chapter to the Academy Sheets as you complete your Academy Notebook.

For God so loved the world,
that He gave His only begotten Son,
that whoever believes in Him
shall not perish, but have eternal life.

CSI Assignment

When something bad occurs, we often wonder why God would allow it, but the Bible says that God takes *all* the circumstances of our lives, even the difficult ones, to create something *good.*

Read Romans 8:28. "And we know that God causes all things to _____ to those who love God, to those who are called according to His purpose."

"I want you to notice two things about this passage," says Jeffries. "First, it says something important—God loves the world. He loves *you*, Jason, and your family."

"Then why did He allow the people in my family to die like they did?" asks Jason.

"I think part of the answer is in the last sentence here: those who love God and believe in Him have *eternal life*."

"What does that mean—to have *eternal life*?" asks Daniel.

"According to the Bible," answers Jeffries, "we're not just physical objects that live for a short time in the universe. We are *living souls*, and we can live even after we die—*forever in heaven*."

Jason still has a doubtful expression. "Are you saying my grandpa isn't really dead?"

"Your grandpa Ren's life here on Earth is over, but the Bible says his soul survives with God, even *now*. In fact, the Bible says you can see your grandpa again, because the real *him*, the *living soul* you know as Ren, is waiting for you after you die."

"My cousin died when I was small," says Hannah. "And I can't wait to see her again."

Jason still doesn't look convinced. "But that doesn't explain why my grandpa had to die the *way* he died. Grandma Miri said he was in pain every day. It just seems wrong—and *cruel*."

Everyone looks at Detective Jeffries. Jason's question is a good one—you also wonder why God would allow Grandpa Ren to suffer. Jeffries takes a deep breath and says, "That's a tough question to answer, but did you hear what Grandma Miri said about the *way* that your grandpa responded to the cancer?"

"What do you mean?" asks Jason.

"Your grandmother said that your grandpa Ren was 'incredibly courageous and calm,'" says Jeffries. "He sounds like an amazing man, and I bet everyone here admires his courage."

All the cadets nod their heads and encourage Jason about how brave his grandpa was.

"Everyone agrees that courage is a good thing," continues Jeffries. "We want to see *more* of it in our world, not *less*. We also want to see more *compassion*, *forgiveness*, and *charity*, right?"

"Sure," says Jason.

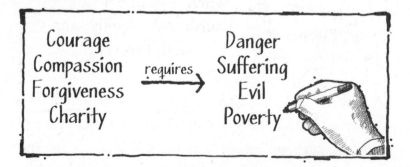

"But if God wanted to develop those *good* attributes in all of us," says Jeffries, "He'd have to allow *bad* things to happen. You can't be *courageous* unless you are responding to *danger*. You can't be *compassionate* unless it's in response to *suffering*. You can't be *forgiving* unless you've been *wronged*. You can't be *charitable* unless someone is *poor*."

Jason looks like he's still not sure what to think.

"Let me put it this way," tries Jeffries again. "If God wanted those *good* things to exist—courage, compassion, forgiveness, and charity—He'd have to allow these *bad* things: danger, suffering, evildoing, and poverty. And He might allow these bad things to happen during our short lives in the universe if He knows we are going to have a wonderful *eternal life*."

"Whatever happens to us here," adds Hannah, "won't compare to how happy we will be when we are reunited with our family and God *forever*."

"Whatever happens to us here won't compare to how happy we will be when we are reunited with our family and God forever."

"That's right," says Jeffries.

"I don't know ..." says Jason. "That's a lot to think about."

"Let me add one *more* thing to think about," says Jeffries, as he stands up and approaches the whiteboard. "You said you thought it was 'wrong' that your grandpa had to die so painfully, and I agree with you. But when you said it was *wrong*, did you mean it was *really* wrong or that it was *your opinion* that it was wrong?"

"This sounds like the session when we talked about *moral truth*," remembers Daniel.

"Exactly," confirms Jeffries. "Right and wrong, good and bad— are these just opinions that people, countries, or planets have, or are they bigger than that?"

"Well, I don't think it's just an *opinion* ..." says Jason.

"If it's not a matter of opinion," says Jeffries, "if it's bigger than that, then it requires a standard of good that doesn't change—like opinions do."

"God is a standard of good," says Hannah. "And I learned in church that He *doesn't change*, even when our opinions about things *do*." Jeffries agrees and adds this as the final piece of evidence in his diagram of the universe.

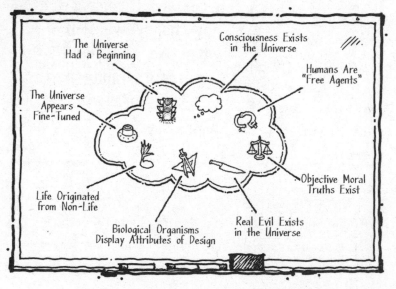

Detective Jeffries opens up the day's final discussion with a question: "When we complain that something seems wrong or bad, we do it because we are comparing things to an unchanging standard of *good*. Where does that standard of good come from?"

"God," says Jason. He seems to be surprised by his own response.

Jeffries smiles. "The presence of evil in the universe," he says as he points to the diagram, "is actually evidence that God *exists*, because without God, there would be no reasonable way to call *anything* evil. Without God as the standard, good and bad are just a matter of opinion."

Jeffries turns to the cadets. "We accomplished a *lot* today. Go home and I'll see you next week. I think we can close these two cases in time for you to graduate from the Special Investigations Academy."

A "Tool" for Your

Detective Bag!
Test Your Conclusions

Detectives aren't afraid to test their conclusions by examining all the different possible explanations for the evidence they've gathered. We want to make sure our conclusions are true.

You may hear different explanations for the eight pieces of evidence in the universe. Don't let that surprise you. Once you examine these different explanations, you'll discover the Christian explanation is true.

Jason and his grandmother take flowers to Ren's grave.

Mysteries Solved

Jason and his grandmother take flowers to Ren's grave. After Grandma Miri places them by the headstone, Jason sits on the ground and begins to speak.

"Grandpa Ren, you've said a lot to me, even without being here. Now I want to say something *to you*. I'm reading your Bible with Grandma. We've been learning about Jesus from the gospel of John. I'm starting to see things differently. I never thought God existed, but I've changed my mind, just like you knew I would. I love you, Grandpa."

As they turn to leave, Jason says, "I've made a decision—a big one."

"Me too," says Grandma.

At the final session of the Special Investigations Academy, Jeffries calls up each cadet to receive his or her graduation certificate.

"In this Academy," says Jeffries, "we learned many new detective skills. We solved the mystery of the shoebox, and we even examined the evidence in the universe." Jeffries smiles at the group of cadets. "You all did a great job," he says sincerely.

Jeffries turns to the whiteboard one last time and sketches the shoebox and his diagram of the universe. First, he points to his drawing of the shoebox.

"We investigated the shoebox and concluded that the evidence *inside the box* was best explained by someone *outside the box*—Grandpa Ren."

"We *did* have some help from the notes that he left us," observes Daniel.

"That's true," says Jeffries, as he points to the diagram of the universe. "We also investigated the universe and concluded that the evidence *inside the cosmos* was best explained by someone *outside*—God."

"We could have used the note that *He* left us," says Hannah, pointing to Grandpa Ren's Bible on the table next to Jason.

"Ha!" laughs Detective Jeffries. "Yes, I guess we could have done that; God does have a lot to say in the Bible about how He created and fine-tuned the universe. But I wanted you to investigate the universe like a crime scene *without* using the Bible. I wanted you to understand why God says everyone should believe He exists, even if they *don't* have a Bible. In a passage written to Christians in Rome, the apostle Paul wrote: 'For since the creation of the world

His invisible attributes, His eternal power and divine nature, have been clearly seen, being understood through what has been made, so that they are without excuse.'"

Jeffries points to the final *Suspect Profile*.

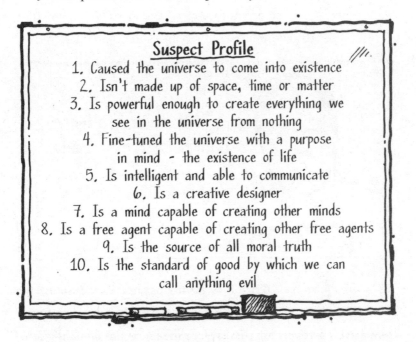

Suspect Profile
1. Caused the universe to come into existence
2. Isn't made up of space, time or matter
3. Is powerful enough to create everything we see in the universe from nothing
4. Fine-tuned the universe with a purpose in mind – the existence of life
5. Is intelligent and able to communicate
6. Is a creative designer
7. Is a mind capable of creating other minds
8. Is a free agent capable of creating other free agents
9. Is the source of all moral truth
10. Is the standard of good by which we can call anything evil

"Everyone should know that God exists, just from the evidence we find in the universe. Based on our investigation, we know a lot about God even *without* His book to us."

Jeffries puts down his marker and looks at Jason. "But now that you have a Bible, Jason, you can learn even more."

"About that ..." says Jason, as everyone turns his way. "In the first Academy Course, we learned about Jesus and what the Bible says about Him. I'll be honest—I almost became a Christian when we finished."

"What stopped you?" asks Hannah.

"I guess a couple things. I still sometimes think miracles are hard to believe, and there are a bunch of them in the Bible. But I was also … mad, I guess. Mad that my parents and grandpa died. And I thought, if there is a God, I'm *mad at Him*."

The cadets listen intently.

Jason continues, "But this Academy has helped me change my mind. If God can create everything in the universe from *nothing*, I know He could easily raise Jesus from the grave and do all the other miracles described in the Bible."

"It's easier to walk on water than it is to create the entire universe!" says Hannah about one of Jesus's more famous miracles.

Jason laughs. "Yes, and I think our talk about evil helped me understand why God would allow my grandpa to die the way he did. If everything hadn't happened the way it did, who knows if I would have taken the Bible seriously?"

"What do you mean, Jason?" asks Jeffries.

"I've been talking with my grandma, and we think God might have used everything in our lives to do something *good*. My parents and my grandpa never stopped believing in Jesus, and my grandpa found a way to get my attention about the Bible. God took care of us all these years, even without Grandpa Ren—and we both have a lot to be thankful for."

Dig Deep
Visit the
Online Academy

By now you should have completed the Activity Sheets and Fill-Ins, so be sure to watch the last video and print out the graduation certificate (or use the one at the end of this book)!

A broad smile slowly spreads on Detective Jeffries's face.

"We made a decision this week," says Jason. "Grandpa Ren said I needed to 'change my mind,' and now I understand what he was talking about. Grandma and I have changed our minds about *two* things."

"Go on, go on," encourages Jeffries.

"We've changed our minds about God. We now believe He exists and we know His name is *Jesus*."

"That's *one* decision," says Jeffries. "What's the other?"

"After reading what the Bible says," continues Jason, "we think we need to change our minds about *us*."

"I don't get it," says Daniel. "What do you mean?"

"I used to think that I was a basically *good* person," starts Jason. "But then I read about Jesus. The more that I read, the more I realize I am far from being perfect. In fact, I'm not even all that *good*."

Jason holds up his grandpa's Bible.

Jason holds up his grandpa's Bible. "There's a word in here: *sin*. I'd heard it before, but *now* I understand it. God made us to be *perfect*, to have no flaws at all, but we aren't. We're … *rebellious*. We want to do things our way instead of God's way. It's not just the things we *do*; it's even the things we *think*."

Jason looks at Detective Jeffries. "You talked about it when we were examining the universe. God is the perfect standard of good. We are not. We are all *imperfect*. So, it makes sense that if we want to live with Him forever, we have to solve that problem."

"So, you decided to be perfect?" asks Daniel. He's not trying to be funny; he just seems like he's trying to understand.

"No," says Jason. "I know I could *never* be perfect. But God has a solution. That's why I think my grandpa wanted me to read John 3:16. God sent Himself in the form of a human, Jesus. He lived a *perfect* life but was killed as though He committed all the sins in the world. If we believe in Him, and that He died on the cross to pay the price for our sins, God will accept *us* as perfect, even though we aren't."

"Jesus took *our punishment*, and we get *His reward*—and it's all for free," adds Jeffries.

"This week," says Jason, "my grandma and I are going to church. It will be my first time, and her first time in many years. We want to tell everyone that we're Christians—and we want to learn more about Jesus."

Jason takes his grandpa's ring from his pocket and puts it on his finger. It dangles loosely. "And someday, I want to earn a ring, just like this one."

The detective places a hand on Jason's shoulder and says, "I believe you'll get that chance, Jason—and opportunities of many other kinds. You're becoming a good detective, and your investigative skills will help you along the way."

CSI Assignment

God offers us eternal life for free, if we will simply admit that we need a Savior and accept what Jesus did for us on the cross.

Read Romans 10:9-10. "If you confess with your mouth _____, and believe in your heart that God

_____, you will be saved; for with the heart a person believes, resulting in _____, and with the mouth he confesses, resulting in _____."

INSTRUCTIONS FOR USING THE WEBSITE

Be sure to visit www.GodsCrimeSceneforKids.com with your parents to watch the videos for each chapter, download the Fill-In and Activity Sheets, and learn how to earn your Academy Graduation Certificate.

As part of your academy training, be sure to complete the Fill-In Sheets for each chapter.

Here are a few of the questions:

Sample Fill-In:

Chapter 1 Note Sheet - How Did It Get Here?
God's Crime Scene for Kids

" _____ is not a good detective skill," says Jeffries.

Why does Detective Jeffries say, "None of you saw that," After picking up Simba?

_____

_____

In the attic, Detective Jeffries puts on a pair of _____ and pulls a _____ from his black detective bag.

One of the first questions an investigator asks, once he or she discovers what might be evidence, is:

_____

Why is it more reasonable to believe that the shoebox came from outside the attic rather than inside the attic?

_____

_____

Sample Fill-In:

Chapter 2 Note Sheet - All Tuned Up
God's Crime Scene for Kids

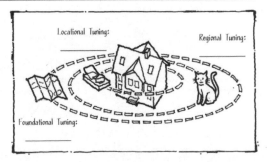

What do the cadets see when they look closely at the shoebox in the Crime Lab?

_____

Why does Detective Jeffries say that Jason's house was "fine-tuned"?

_____

Write in the layers of fine tuning in the diagrams:

Now think about the universe. Detective Jeffries says, "Now let's look at the three levels of fine-tuning we've discovered. Could something _____ the universe have caused everything to be _____?"

Locational Tuning:
_____

Regional Tuning:
_____

Foundational Tuning:

Sample Fill-In:

Chapter 3 Note Sheet - Directions for Life
God's Crime Scene for Kids

Two items in the shoebox are different than the rest because they contain _____ . "Artists are _____ , just like authors."

Who is the boy in the drawing? _____

What does Jason say about the tree in the drawing? _____

What kind of tree is it? _____
Where did it come from? _____
Why was it planted? _____
How did it get in Jason's Yard? _____
Who planted the tree? _____

Now, think about the universe, "All the _____ in our universe; everything on our planet from bacteria, to plants like Jason's Maple tree, to animals like Simba and even humans like all of us in this room - these living things came from _____."

Sample Fill-In:

Chapter 4 Note Sheet - The Obvious Artist
God's Crime Scene for Kids

Fill in the diagram of Jasmine's nest adding the evidence that shows it was designed by birds:

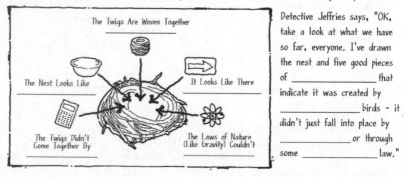

The Twigs Are Woven Together

The Nest Looks Like

It Looks Like There

The Twigs Didn't Come Together By

The Laws of Nature (Like Gravity) Couldn't

Detective Jeffries says, "OK, take a look at what we have so far, everyone. I've drawn the nest and five good pieces of _____ that indicate it was created by _____ birds - it didn't just fall into place by _____ or through some _____ law."

Jeffries draws a microscopic motor called a: _____

Sample Fill-In:
Chapter 5 Note Sheet - Thinking about Thinking
God's Crime Scene for Kids

Dr. Kelley says, "I'm a licensed _____ , just like the kind of doctor you visit when you are sick, only I have a specialty: _____."

Detective Jeffries brought the cadets to the Coroner's Office to learn the difference between our _____ and _____ so they can understand what they are using when they _____."

Dr. Kelley says, "Sometimes people mistakenly think your _____ is the same thing as your _____, but it's not. For example, you can _____ a brain in your hands. You can even put it in a _____!"

Sample Fill-In:
Chapter 6 Note Sheet - A Change of Mind
God's Crime Scene for Kids

What does Hannah see in Grandma Miri's flower bed?

_____

Why do the cadets think this discovery is related to the mystery of the shoebox?

_____

_____

"We can't just _____ Grandma Miri's flower bed." Hannah looks at Jason, "I mean, not until we at least get her _____."

"Well," says Jeffries, "You may have discovered important _____ in that yard - evidence that might help us solve the mystery of the _____ and the mystery of the _____."

"If everything that happens in our _____ is purely physical, the activity between your _____ is just like this row of _____." He pushes the first domino and all the others fall in sequence... "Could any of these dominoes choose _____ fall?" he asks.

Sample Fill-In:
Chapter 7 Note Sheet - Choosing Right from Wrong
God's Crime Scene for Kids

Detective Jeffries tells the cadets that they recognized an important moral truth while waiting for Grandma Miri. What is it?

_____

_____

"I'm so glad you waited to ask me about _____ my flowers," says Grandma Miri, "Just do your best not to _____ too many of these beauties as you _____ your mystery."

What do the cadets discover in the flowerbed? What does it contain?

_____

_____

Why aren't moral truths just a matter of personal opinion?

_____

_____

Sample Fill-In:
Chapter 8 Note Sheet - Good News about Bad Things
God's Crime Scene for Kids

Why is the study Grandma Miri's happiest and saddest place?

_____

_____

_____

Grandma Miri says, "My faith was _____. Ren always said that God is love, but I couldn't _____ that anymore. I just stopped believing in God altogether."

"Lots of people have questioned why an all-_____, all-_____ God would allow _____ to occur in the universe," says Jeffries to all the cadets.

"But if there's more to _____ than just what happens to us here in the _____, it might explain why God allows things to happen to us - even bad things."